STITCHING · HISTORY · FROM THE HOLOCAUST

Book design by Barbara Budish,
Sr. Graphic Designer, Milwaukee Jewish Federation

Library of Congress Cataloging-in-Publication Data

Jewish Museum Milwaukee, a program of the Milwaukee Jewish Federation
Stitching History From the Holocaust/Jewish Museum Milwaukee
52p.
ISBN 0-692-28397-4
1. Holocaust, Jewish (1939-1945) 2. Fashion Design – Czechoslovakia 3. Strnad Family
I. Jewish Museum Milwaukee   II. Title

PRINTED IN THE UNITED STATES OF AMERICA

First Edition: September 2014

This project is dedicated
to all the people and talent lost in the Holocaust

Acknowledgements

This exhibit was created by Jewish Museum Milwaukee
Penny Deshur, *President*
Marianne Lubar, *Exhibit Chair*

Jewish Museum Milwaukee Exhibit Staff
Kathie Bernstein, *Executive Director*
Molly Dubin, *Curator*
Ellie Gettinger, *Education Director*
Jay Hyland, *Archives Director*
Jane A. Avner, *Historical Researcher*
Hannah Lartz, *Administrative Assistant*
Tyler D. Grasee, *Intern*

Jeff Jones, *Marketing & Communications Manager*
Barbara Budish, *Sr. Graphic Designer*
Melissa Taylor, *Social Media Coordinator*

Exhibit Sponsors

Jewish Museum Milwaukee is grateful to the following for their generous support of the exhibition and this catalog:

Anonymous
The Brico Fund
The Lynde & Harry Bradley Foundation
Daniel M. Soref Charitable Trust
Penny & James Deshur
Evan & Marion Helfaer Charitable Trust
Herzfeld Foundation
Suzy Ettinger
Helen & Ronald Jacobs
Marianne & Sheldon Lubar
Sue & Bud Selig
The Strnad Family

This exhibit was funded in part by a grant from the Wisconsin Humanities Council, with funds from the National Endowment for the Humanities and the State of Wisconsin. Any views, findings, conclusions or recommendations expressed in this project do not necessarily represent those of the National Endowment for the Humanities. The Wisconsin Humanities Council supports and creates programs that use history, culture, and discussion to strengthen community life for everyone in Wisconsin.

This project is funded in part through a grant from the City of Milwaukee Arts Board and the Wisconsin Arts Board.

Exhibit Co-Sponsor
The Nathan & Esther Pelz Holocaust Education Resource Center

Table of Contents

Honoring Loss Through History and Creativity:
The Curator's Viewpoint

by Molly Dubin

Creating exhibits is one of the greatest privileges in the world of museum work. It is an energizing and challenging undertaking which is much like putting together a puzzle. There can be many pieces, and while each separate component may stand alone with distinct merit and meaning, when pieced together, the whole takes on a greater significance – establishing connections and revealing unexpected consequences. Telling a story requires research, artifact selection, gallery design, and a compelling narrative – elements brought together through unique collaborations and resources to make this important project possible.

In the case of Hedwig ('Hedy') and Paul Strnad, the primary facts of their lives were included in the Jewish Museum Milwaukee's permanent exhibit when it opened in 2008. While the Holocaust and other sections of the permanent exhibit are comprised of materials culled from local organizations and families, the information and lessons presented are universal in reach and implication. Key events and concepts are addressed in terms of their impact on Milwaukee's Jewish community and expanded on to address national and global vantage points. The Strnad story is no exception. Paul's plea for help to escape Nazi persecution, sent to his cousin Alvin in Milwaukee, struck a particularly poignant chord with Museum staff and visitors alike. Accompanying that letter were dress designs by Paul's wife, Hedwig, included for the purpose of demonstrating her ability to be viably employed in the United States. This intimate knowledge strengthens our ability to recognize the experiences of our own relatives through the Strnads' prism. While placing the horrors of the Holocaust in our own backyard, it also revealed another significant story. Along with the loss of six million Jewish lives, an incalculable amount of talent and creativity was extinguished – never to be realized.

To develop an exhibition over 70 years after Hedwig and Paul Strnad became victims of Nazi genocide, the Museum brought Hedy's designs to fruition. While the ensembles at the core of the exhibit provide an opportunity to demonstrate that a vast void can never be filled, they also breathe life into creations which otherwise would never have seen the light of day. Through this original exhibit, *Stitching History From the Holocaust*, new artifacts become part of a legacy of memory, to be protected by and shared with future generations.

Molly Dubin is the Curator of the Jewish Museum Milwaukee, where she develops and organizes exhibits and programs. She holds a master's degree in Art History and Museum Studies from the University of Denver and has worked in the fields of art and Judaic enrichment for over 20 years.

December 11, 1939.

Dear Alvin:

I received your last letter and thank you very much for your kind care. I was very glad to hear, that you are troubling to get an affidavit of necessity for my wife as a dress-designer. Would you be so kind as to let me know if you have had any success in this matter. You may imagine that we have a great interest of leaving Europe as soon as possible, because there is no possibility of getting a position in this country. By seperate mail I have sent you some dress-designs my wife made. I hope the dress-manufacturer you mentioned in your letter will like them.

As to my family I can inform you that we all are well. All the members have lost their employments and can not find any work. I am helping my wife in shopping and making artificial lether and silk flowers, which are much in favor here.

Could I trouble you to send me a fashion-journal (for ladies), because we can not get them now from Paris and are not informed about Paris fashions. Many thanks for your kindness beforehand.

I had the intention to send you the new stamps of the Protektorat Bohemia and Moravia, but I could not do so, because it is forbidden now to send stamps to your country.

Hoping to hear very soon from you I remain with kind regards to you and your wife and with the best wishes for the New Year

Yours sincerely
Paul

P.S. Enclosed you find a photo of both of us.

Introduction

by Jane A. Avner

"You may imagine that we have a great interest of leaving Europe as soon as possible."

– December 11, 1939

In 1939, Paul Strnad (1895-1943), resident of Prague, Czechoslovakia, wrote these understated words to his cousin Alvin Strnad (1904-1968) who lived in Milwaukee, Wisconsin. Neither had any illusions about the danger the Nazi regime in Germany posed to Europe's Jewish population.

Although Jews were a recognized minority with full citizenship in Czechoslovakia, the 1938 Munich Agreement had allowed Germany to appropriate the Sudetenland (a strip of land bordering Germany), and in March 1939, the Germans had invaded all of Czechoslovakia. The *Wisconsin Jewish Chronicle* diligently reported on March 24, "Anti-Jewish Campaign Sweeps over Territory in Reich 'Protectorate'," noting seizure of community funds, arrests, suicides and the expected implementation of the discriminatory Nuremberg Laws denying Jews the most basic human rights.

Late in 1939 Alvin attempted to bring his cousin Paul and his wife Hedwig (1899-1943) from Prague to America. He opened a file at the U.S. State Department to obtain visas for them. Although Paul had lost his job, Hedwig was able to continue doing piecework. Paul sent Alvin samples of Hedwig's dress designs to convince someone – anyone – that the Prague Strnads would not be a drain on the U.S. economy should some company or manufacturer only give them a chance.

There were so many who wanted to escape, but too few visas would be issued due to the restrictive U.S. immigration laws, a byproduct of nativism, the ongoing economic depression, and fear. Paul, Hedwig, Hedwig's mother, Paul's father, and his three sisters were all transported to the Czech concentration camp Theresienstadt and then on to other ghettos and concentration camps where they all died.

The letter and the samples of Hedwig's dress designs remained in Alvin Strnad's Milwaukee home. Alvin passed away in 1968 and his son Burton Strnad (1930-2009) was unaware of their existence until he was cleaning out his father's home and found the letter and drawings in the family home's basement.

Hedwig and Paul Strnad in the picture they sent to Alvin in 1939.

The precious items were generously donated to the Milwaukee Jewish Archives in 1997 and became an integral part of the Holocaust area of the Jewish Museum Milwaukee, which opened in 2008. The emotionally charged letter juxtaposed with the charm of the fashionable sketches haunted visitors and museum professionals alike. One suggested, "Why don't you create Hedwig's dresses and tell her story?"

The sequence of events was powerful, and it wove together themes that resonate today: prejudice, the role of women, fashion history, persecution, immigration, and local history on two continents. But the narrative was still rather thin. We had to learn more before we were ready to mount an exhibit.

The byproduct of any research project is discovery. New information about Hedwig Strnad and her family emerged from three continents. Beginning with the Yad Vashem research facilities in Jerusalem and the Holocaust databases in the Czech Republic, we were able to pinpoint precisely when Hedwig, Paul and their family were deported to the Theresienstadt concentration camp and from there to other ghettos and concentration camps. We learned more about the families from a dedicated researcher in Prague, Dana Martin. She also discovered from where in Bohemia the Strnad family originated, and that Hedwig had two sisters. With our concurrent research on the American path of the Strnads, our understanding of the immigration experience was deepened considerably. Our most startling and moving discoveries came in 2014, the year our exhibit opened. We knew that Paul and Hedwig's niece had survived the Holocaust, but we could not locate her. During the winter of 2014, Tyler Grasee, a Lawrence University student interning in Berlin, succeeded where we had failed. He contacted her, interviewed her in her home in Nuremberg, and further helped us to understand her aunt, the woman behind the sketches. Then, in the summer of 2014, as we were preparing this catalog and the panels for the exhibit, the Milwaukee Strnads found a container that had been placed in storage after the death of Burton Strnad, the original donor of the material. In it were precious historical photographs of Strnads from both sides of the ocean, and most astonishingly, a letter from Paul Strnad to Alvin – the same correspondents – dated October 28, 1938, right after the Munich Pact. This letter shed more light on the Strnad family's feelings that their country's supposed allies had betrayed them; that Jews were in terrible danger; and that they wanted to immigrate to the United States. It also finally established that Hedwig Strnad was an independent dressmaker with a shop of her own, something that her niece had remembered, but was now verified.

Stitching History From the Holocaust: The Life of Hedwig Strnad is a collaboration of the Jewish Museum Milwaukee, the Milwaukee Repertory Theater, and scholars in the fields of American and European Jewish History, the Holocaust, Women's History, and Fashion Design. The endeavor is supported by private and public grants. It has been constructed so that after its opening at the Jewish Museum Milwaukee, it can be loaned to other institutions where its multiple themes can be explored by numerous audiences.

This catalog consists of nine essays. Seven are written by scholars and professionals who responded to the Strnad story as we initially knew it within their areas of expertise. It should be noted that these essays were written before the discoveries described above. One essay recounts the step-by-step realization of the Hedwig Strnad drawings by the Milwaukee Repertory Theater Costume Shop, meticulously crafted in 2014. The ninth essay discusses the interview with Paul and Hedwig's niece which was conducted in February 2014. The catalog includes a letter from Alvin's granddaughter, Karen Strnad to Hedwig's living niece, Brigitte Neumann Rohaczek. Hedwig's sketches and other illustrations will also be found within the catalog.

With the exhibit and this catalog, it is our intention that Hedwig Strnad, her talent, and her story, will not be forgotten.

Strands of Memory

by Rachel N. Baum

The story of Hedwig and Paul Strnad is all too familiar. A Jewish couple tries desperately to escape Nazi terror, but cannot, and is ultimately killed along with most of their extended family. The repetition of this story does not dull its anguish, but rather magnifies it.

All too little is known about Hedwig Strnad, and in this too, the Strnads are like so many victims of the Holocaust. While the Strnads had family in the United States who gave the few items they had to a museum, most did not have even this.

The materials left behind hardly seem enough to form the basis of an exhibit: one letter, eight dress designs, and the barest of information about the Strnad's Holocaust experiences. The sparseness of the artifacts pushes against the visitor's expectations of a Holocaust exhibit. We traditionally come to a Holocaust exhibit to see the past represented, to have some of our questions answered, to learn. Here, however, the exhibit raises more questions than it answers.

The subject of the exhibit is the very act of memory, and in this, the visitor cannot be passive. One does not simply "take in" this exhibit; one must choose to be part of it. Looking at the small number of artifacts, the visitor must ask: What should be done with these materials, these echoes of a life? How should a person such as Hedwig Strnad be mourned? What does it mean to be a good steward of Holocaust memory?

Answering such questions requires visitors to consider the complexities of Holocaust memory. There is not one "memory" which should be remembered and repeated. Rather, the act of memory is an act of stitching together an understanding of the past and giving it contemporary meaning. It is the process by which the Holocaust is conceptualized, understood, and represented.

In the case of Hedwig Strnad, the threads are utterly thin. The materials of the exhibit scream in their insufficiency. *This is what is left.* This is what is left – what is known – about the life of a forty-three year old woman.

There are no diaries to read, no reflections of her inner life. The visitor confronts an image *of* Hedwig and images *by* Hedwig, but there are no words. This absence of Hedwig's own voice is significant, since the most that

Hedwig Strnad's photograph from Yad Vashem Page of Testimony submitted by her niece after the war.

12

scholars and visitors to the exhibit can add is the broader historical and cultural context. Historical and cultural context gives shape to an individual life, but it is not a life. The exhibit has eight dress designs, but as visitors try to create a sense of Hedwig Strnad, they are left with scraps of material, without a pattern to follow.

Piecing together memory from what is here requires looking not only at the exhibits, but looking as well at the absences, being attentive to what is not here. What can we *not* know about Hedwig Strnad? Even the exact date of her death is missing.

We know that Hedwig was a dress designer, but we do not know, for example, if she wanted children. Did she turn away from motherhood for other aims, or was she unable to have children? The answer to this single question would give us valuable information about the life she envisioned for herself, the possibilities that were taken from her.

The silences that surround Hedwig's life encompass not only her pre-Holocaust life, but her experiences during the Shoah as well. What was life like for her in the four months she was at Theresienstadt? We know that many of the prisoners of Theresienstadt were artists, but we cannot know with whom Hedwig met, whether she found ways to sketch, whether she was able to hold onto hope.

Stitching together a life requires considering the multiple threads that affected the particular design of an individual's experiences. Even a very broad historiography of the events that affected Hedwig's Holocaust experiences might look like this:

- **July 6 – 15, 1938.** Evian Conference. Delegates from 32 countries and representatives from relief organizations meet in Evian, France, to discuss the plight of the German-Jewish refugees. Despite expressing sympathy for them, most countries, including the United States and Britain, are unwilling to accept more immigration.

- **September 29 – 30, 1938.** Munich Pact. Leaders from Great Britain, France, Italy, and Germany meet in Munich. In exchange for Hitler's pledge of peace, the countries agree to allow Germany to annex the Sudetenland. Hitler saw this as a "return" of ethnic Germans and their land to Germany.

- **October 1938.** German troops enter the Sudetenland, home to Paul Strnad's family. More than 20,000 Jews who live there flee to the Czech provinces of Bohemia and Moravia.

- **November 9 – 10, 1938**. *Kristallnacht* (Night of the Broken Glass). Anti-Jewish pogroms spread violence and terror throughout the German Reich, including in the Sudetenland. Hundreds of synagogues and Jewish-owned businesses are destroyed. Storm troopers attack Jews in the street.

- **1938 – 1940.** In response to *Kristallnacht*, Great Britain eases immigration restrictions for some Jewish refugees. Kindertransport efforts bring thousands of Jewish children to Great Britain, including Brigitte Neumann, Paul Strnad's niece.

- **December 11, 1939.** Paul Strnad writes to his cousin Alvin in Milwaukee, in the hopes that he can find a way to bring them to the U.S.

- **January 20, 1942.** Fifteen high-ranking Nazi Party and German government officials meet in Wannsee to plan the "Final Solution of the Jewish Question."

- **February 12, 1942.** Hedwig Strnad is deported to Theresienstadt.

- **April 25, 1942.** Hedwig Strnad is transported from Theresienstadt to the Warsaw Ghetto.

- **September 1942.** The ghetto population, which at one time was as high as 450,000, is drastically reduced by disease and malnutrition. Mass deportations commence during the summer reducing the population to 70,000.

- **January 1943.** German SS and police units deport approximately 6,500 Jewish residents of the Warsaw ghetto to Treblinka.

- **April 19 - May 16, 1943.** German SS and police forces "clear" the Warsaw Ghetto, in an operation they called "liquidation." They are met by Jewish resistance that will later be known as the Warsaw ghetto uprising. The German forces kill more than 7,000 Jews, most of them resistance fighters and people in hiding. Approximately 7,000 more Jews are deported to Treblinka and about 42,000 to concentration camps and forced-labor camps.

We know that Hedwig was a dress designer, but we do not know, for example, if she wanted children. Did she turn away from motherhood for other aims, or was she unable to have children? The answer to this single question would give us valuable information about the life she envisioned for herself, the possibilities that were taken from her.

The little we know about Hedwig comes from the testimony given to Yad Vashem by her niece, Brigitte (Neumann) Rohaczek. She escaped the fate of her family because she was sent on a Kindertransport to safety in Great Britain. In her testimony, Brigitte Rohaczek says that the last news from or of Hedwig Strnad came in 1943, from Warsaw. The last information that Yad Vashem has of her is her name on the trans-port of Jews sent to the Warsaw Ghetto in 1942. Did Strnad in fact live to 1943? To what news does

Mrs. Rohaczek refer? Her testimony given to Yad Vashem cries out with questions. Mrs. Rohaczek imagines that Hedwig Strnad might have been sent to Treblinka or to Auschwitz, but then she suggests that Hedwig most probably died in Warsaw. There is something oddly hopeful in Mrs. Rohaczek's thought that Hedwig might have survived long enough to be transported to Treblinka, although the reality is that an earlier death would have spared her more anguish. Facing this lack of clarity about Hedwig's death forces the visitor to squarely face the brutality and horror of the Holocaust – not because we must see Hedwig's death in a photograph, but because there is nothing to see. Hedwig, like so many others, has been denied even a place and a date for her passing.

The two dates given on a gravestone represent the significance of a life. They say, *here lies a human being who walked the earth and mattered to someone*. For Holocaust victims denied such a stone, it is we who must offer the sense of significance. We are not, after all, stewards of Holocaust memory as much as we are creators of it. The scholar James Young, who has written extensively about Holocaust museums and memorials, writes that the art of Holocaust memory "neither begins with a monument's ground-breaking nor ends with the ceremonies conducted at its base. Rather, this art consists in the ongoing activity of memory, in the debates surrounding these memorials, in our own participation in the memorial's performance. For, in the end, we must also realize that the art of memory remains incomplete,

an empty exercise, until visitors have grasped – and then responded to – current suffering in the world in light of a remembered past" (38).

We have only strands of the life of dressmaker Hedwig Strnad. Yet if you take the letters of "strand" and rearrange them, you find: Strnad.

This is the work of memory: taking threads and stitching them together to give shape to what was lost, and stitching that further into our lives. The exhibit on Hedwig and Paul Strnad invites visitors to debate the meaning and interpretations of the artifacts, to consider what it means to remember the Holocaust, and, ultimately, to be changed by this connection with one of the millions of unknown lives lost in the Shoah.

Postscript: In the Fall of 2013, the Jewish Museum Milwaukee employed an intern, Tyler Grasee, who dedicated himself to finding the Strnad's niece, Brigitte Rohaczek. Because he was living in Germany, Tyler was able to interview Mrs. Rohaczek about the Strnads. Mrs. Rohaczek is in her 80s; had the Museum waited to mount this exhibit, Mrs. Rohaczek's memories might have been lost forever. Instead, however, we have precious recordings of Mrs. Rohaczek speaking with affection of her aunt and uncle. We learn that Paul and Hedy were great fun and that they owned a puppet theater.

Mrs. Rohaczek has photos of Hedwig and Paul, and the Museum is hoping that they can be scanned and sent to the Museum. I hope that by the time these words are read, the photographs are part of the ever-developing exhibit of Hedy Strnad's life. With each new piece, our knowledge of Hedy Strnad becomes stronger, and we are better able to mourn her as a specific person.

In the summer of 2014, the museum received a new letter from a relative of the Strnads. [note: the letter follows this essay] This letter predates the letter mentioned in my essay, the letter that began this entire exhibit. In the new letter, Paul expresses how difficult their situation has become and how much they need to leave Europe. He writes, "Please do not be annoyed that i [sic] trouble you with this matter, but if you yourself were here and could see things with your own eyes I am sure you would understand why I make such a request." When I saw this letter, I wept – both for its discovery, and for all that was taken from Paul and Hedy. Reading it makes the next letter – the one with the dress designs – all the more desperate and important.

When I first saw the images of Hedy's designs, I could not imagine the woman whose hands drew them. With these latest miraculous discoveries, the palpable presence of Hedy Strnad takes shape. She was not saved from death, but because of the work of the Jewish Museum Milwaukee, she has been saved from oblivion.

Information submitted by Hedwig's niece, Brigitte Neumann Rohaczek, to Yad Vashem in Jerusalem.

Sources

James Young, ed. *The Art of Memory: Holocaust Memorials in History.* Munich: Pestel-Verlag, 1994.

United States Holocaust Memorial Museum, Holocaust Encyclopedia. www.ushmm.org

Rachel N. Baum is an Adjunct Assistant Professor, Department of Foreign Languages and Literature, and Major Coordinator, Sam & Helen Stahl Center for Jewish Studies, University of Wisconsin-Milwaukee

Prague, 24 th of October 38.

Dear Alvin!

I am sorry I was not able recently to send you along any Czechoslovakian stamps, as there have not been any new issues lately. It is not be presumed either that there will be any for some time on account of the recent unhappy events. In any case I am sending you along some stamps of the more recent issues, as I do not remember distinctly wether you have had these already.

You will of course have read in the press what a catastrophe has overtaken our country, a catastrophe which has upset our whole life, which formerly ran so smoothly. Policically deserted by its allies our republic was compelled to help the couse of peace at an all too great loss to itself by giving up a great part of its territory to Germany, Poland und Hungary. My father's home town Aussig has fallen to Germany. Fortunately my father an my sister Erna were able to get away before the town was occupied, but at the cost of leaving behind their entire house property /three houses/ They are living with us here in Prague. An unavoidable consequence of these events will be that the influence of Germany will greatly increase in this country and you can imagine what this will mean to us Jews living here, and how it will threaten our means of livelyhood. Even now strong anti-semitic tentencies are making themselves felt, such tentencies as never even existed before in this country. These tentencies will probably not be able to be kept in bounds and one may even presume that they will spread all over Europe. Nothing will remain thersefore to do but to adapt oneself to the circumstances and to consider emigrating from Europe.

Paul wrote this letter to his cousin a month after the Munich Agreement which gave parts of Czechoslovakia to Nazi Germany. This letter was given to Jewish Museum Milwaukee in July, 2014

I am writing therefore to ask you wether there is a possibility of emigrating to the U.S.A. where I and my wife /we are childless/ might find some occupation. I am 43 years of age and have been for the last 20 years a clerk in a large bank. My wife is 39 and for the last 17 years has been running, as proprietress, a first class dressmaking establishment. She has a number of workpeople and enjoys a very good reputation here in Prague, as she is very diligent , has a first class knowledge of her line and has very good taste. We both know English fairly well, but of course do not speak perfectly, but we are sure that with the knowledge we already have we should soon pick it up. I have heard from acquaintances that to obtain a permit to enter the States one must have a so-called affidavit from an American citizen. As you are yourself a lawyer i am sure that you know all about it and could procure us such a document, so that when we see no other way out of our difficulties we could find work over there. Naturally i should refund all fees connected with the procuring of such an affidavit. Please do not be annoyed that i trouble you with this matter, but if you your-self were herse and could see things with your own eyes I am sure you would understand why I make such a request. You may be quite sure that we shall not be a burden to anybody, as in the first line my wife is sure to find some occupation in her line, and as concerns myself if not just in my own line I should look for any other occupation, even if it were manuel work in the first time.

Hoping that you will not take it amiss that I am making you this request an that you will be able to help me, I remain, with the kindest regards to yourself an your wife an thanking you in advance for any trouble you may be put to,

                                      Yours very sincerely

                                              Paul

Immigration and the Strnad Family: Two Eras, Two Outcomes

by Rachel Ida Buff

This exhibit features artifacts from the Strnad family, whose members lived in Bohemia – then part of the Austro-Hungarian Empire – and the United States. Like most immigrants, the Strnad family maintained connections across oceans and national boundaries. Ongoing contact with families abroad shaped the lives of immigrants in the United States. As the correspondence between Alvin and Paul Strnad poignantly illuminates, these transoceanic connections also became a source of hope for European Jews during the gathering storm of the late 1930s and early 1940s.

The family members who successfully emigrated to the United States came much earlier, during an era of comparatively open migration from Europe. When Benedict and Julius Strnad arrived, in 1891 and 1905 respectively, they were part of a large cohort of immigrants from Southern and Eastern Europe. This group included many Jews, Italians, Greeks, Slavs, Poles and Syrians. Drawn to the comparative social tolerance and the possibility of work in the industrializing country, these newcomers transformed the ethnic and religious makeup of the United States. Many of those who decided to set out for a new country knew something about what to expect there through letters home, advertising from immigration agencies, and the stories told by returning migrants and travelers.

For prospective emigrants who could raise the money for permits and fare, it was fairly easy to obtain passage to the United States from a German or Mediterranean port. There, they were subject to a shipboard inspection by the U.S. Consulate. Arriving in the United States, Julius would have been inspected again at the newly opened immigration station at Ellis Island; Benedict entered the country a year before Ellis Island opened, and likely passed through its predecessor in New York Harbor, Castle Garden.

One and a half million Jews arrived in the United States between 1881 and 1910, primarily from Eastern and Central Europe. Fleeing poverty and persecution in Europe, most of these migrants entered through the

---

Top photo: *Benedict Strnad's first department store on Kinnickinnic Avenue in Milwaukee, 1908.* Jewish Museum Milwaukee

port of New York City. Benedict and Julius left Bohemia, where Jews enjoyed comparative tolerance and success. In migrating, they joined this large cohort in the United States.

Milwaukee's then predominantly German Jewish community responded quickly to the increase of migration, forming an Immigrant Relief Society in 1881. Working with Jewish relief organizations on the East Coast, the Milwaukee Immigrant Relief Society worked to resettle refugees in Milwaukee and small towns in rural Wisconsin. Initially, Jewish, Christian and civic charities collaborated in emergency refugee resettlement.

While some tensions arose among new arrivals and native-born Jews in Milwaukee, the city became a destination for new Jewish arrivals from Europe like Benedict and Julius. They found employment, working as tailors, bakers and house painters; some relied on networks transported from Europe to finance small retail business ventures. New synagogues and other cultural institutions were founded. By 1920, the Jewish population of Milwaukee had grown to 22,000.

But by the time Paul Strnad sought immigration assistance from his cousin Alvin in Milwaukee in 1939, the situation for prospective European migrants had changed dramatically. Where migrants from Julius and Benedict's time found few obstacles, Paul and Hedwig encountered a formidable bureaucracy that ultimately prevented them from escaping deportation and death.

As immigration from Southern and Eastern Europe and Asia increased in the early 20th century, many "native born" Americans, some of them first generation immigrants themselves, became concerned. They feared economic competition, and they claimed that the religious and cultural practices of the new migrants meant that they could never become true Americans. This concern led first to the Chinese Exclusion Act of 1882, and later to "national origins" quotas, which greatly restricted immigration from Southern and Eastern Europe, cutting off migrants from the "Asia-Pacific triangle" stretching from Japan to Afghanistan altogether.

Under the Johnson-Reed Act of 1924, prospective emigrants had to obtain a visa from the U.S. Consulate before purchasing tickets to leave. Throughout the 1930s, few visas were granted, even for "non-quota" immigrants: wives and children of U.S. citizens, ministers, and university professors. Between March of 1938 and September of 1939, approximately 85,000 Jewish refugees managed to reach the United States. In June of 1939, 300,000 applicants sought visas from U.S. consulates in Europe. Few succeeded in obtaining one. Although there is evidence that Alvin Strnad initiated the paperwork to bring his cousins over to the United States, the odds against his succeeding were high.

How was it possible that so many obstacles lay in the path of those seeking refuge from Nazi terror? An earlier tendency to restrict immigration combined with wartime security anxieties in nations that might have sheltered refugees like the Strnads. After *Kristallnacht* in November, 1938, many in Western Europe and the Americas feared a massive influx of refugees. Few nations were prepared to accept large populations of refugees. Further, in May of 1939, Great Britain severely curtailed Jewish entry to Palestine. Starting in 1940, the U.S. Department of State ordered consulates abroad to delay visa approvals.

Some refugees managed to find asylum in Central and South America, and in Japanese-controlled Shanghai, which did not require a visa. Some were able to migrate to Palestine illegally. But like Hedwig and Paul, most found their possibilities for escape quite limited.

American Jews continued to advocate for their relatives abroad. Led by Rabbi Stephen Wise, the American Jewish Congress (AJC) held rallies to protest Nazi policies. The AJC acted as a liaison between the World Jewish Congress and the U.S. State Department, advocating for relief for Jews in Europe. Smaller organizations, along with individuals like Alvin Strnad, deployed mighty efforts on behalf of their relatives in Europe.

In this exhibit, Hedwig Strnad's designs finally find shape as dresses. Their graceful lines remind us of myriad possibilities curtailed by the Holocaust. Possibilities for refuge and rescue also existed across the ocean, but few were realized at the time.

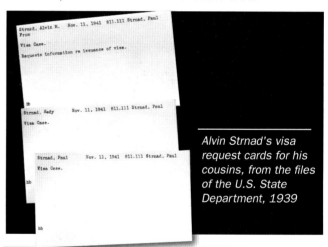

Alvin Strnad's visa request cards for his cousins, from the files of the U.S. State Department, 1939

Sources

Donna R. Gabaccia, *Foreign Relations: American Immigration in Global Perspective.* Princeton, N.J.: Princeton University Press, 2012.

Martin Hintz, *Jewish Milwaukee.* Chicago: Aurora Publishing, 2005.

Dorothee Schneider, *Crossing Borders: Migration and Citizenship in the Twentieth Century United States.* Cambridge: Harvard University Press, 2011.

Louis J. Swichkow and Lloyd P. Gartner, *The History of the Jews of Milwaukee.* Philadelphia: Jewish Publication Society of America, 1963.

United States Holocaust Memorial Museum, Holocaust Encyclopedia, @ www.ushmm.org.

Rachel Ida Buff is an Associate Professor, Department of History, and Coordinator, Comparative Ethnic Studies Program, University of Wisconsin-Milwaukee.

The Jews of Bohemia: A Lesser Known Story

by Shay Pilnik

Bohemia, for several centuries part of the Austrian Habsburg Dynasty, a land inhabited by Jews and Christians, speaking both Czech and German, has often been missing from the scene of European Jewish history. Rather, two centers, one in Eastern Europe and one in the west, have loomed large throughout the twentieth century in Jewish collective memory.

On one pole stood the Polish and Russian center, home of the largest community worldwide and the birthplace of the great Jewish political movements of the modern era (Zionism, Diaspora Nationalism, and Territorialism). On the other pole stood the Western European center: in France, the first country to grant Jews emancipation, and in Germany, home of the great Jewish cultural and theological currents (the Haskalah Movement, Reform Judaism and modern Orthodoxy). This tendency to compare east and west, productive as it may be, has often left the story of the smaller Jewish communities such as Bohemia, inhabiting the center of Europe, out of the spotlight.

Why is the unique story of Bohemian Jews neglected? True, the relatively small size of Bohemia's Jewish population partly accounts for its being eclipsed. At the turn of the twentieth century there were only 27,000

Jews living in Prague, Bohemia's largest Jewish community. But demography aside, both Bohemia and Prague certainly deserve far more attention and recognition as a distinct place in the Jewish people's time-honored history of life in exile.

During the early 18th century, when the number of Jews residing in Prague reached 11,000, the city became the third largest Jewish community of Europe, lagging only behind Amsterdam and Salonika. Prague's Jewish community on the eve of the modern era in European Jewish history was a product of both economic growth and cultural flowering that emerged as early as the 13th century. While Jews are mentioned in descriptions of Prague as early as the mid-tenth century, it was only in 1254 that Pemysl Ottokar II, the king of Bohemia, issued a charter that granted Jews protection, and both religious and judicial autonomy. It included the right to

pay taxes collectively, to supervise the community's internal affairs and to bring Jews to trial in its own rabbinic courts. This charter of privileges, turning the Jewish community into a corporate entity, was later adopted in Hungary, Poland and Lithuania. While the Jews of Bohemia in general, and Prague in particular, were not spared the pogroms that swept central Europe in the late 11th century coming upon the heels of the First Crusade, and attacks associated with accusations of blood libel and blasphemy launched toward the close of the Middle Ages, Bohemia did remain a relatively safe haven for Jews in an otherwise virulently hostile environment.

Thus, Jewish life in the Bohemian capital continued to flourish as the High Middle Ages wore on. Indeed, Prague is one of the only cities in Europe where one could find a continuous Jewish presence, stretching from the Middle Ages until the eve of the Holocaust, with two quite brief incidents of expulsion (between 1557-1564 and 1745-1748). Prague was also a major center of rabbinic scholarship. To demonstrate how relatively amicable Prague was on the medieval central European landscape, we may mention Rabbi Yitshak ben Moshe (1180-1260), Prague's earliest rabbinic luminary, known as 'Or Zarua' ("light is sown"), who used the medieval Czech language in order to clarify textual difficulties in his Talmudic discussions. For a community otherwise insulated from the world outside, speaking its own language (the local Bohemian and Moravian Yiddish dialect, known as böhmisch-mährisches Judendeutsch), and having ties with the non-Jewish world limited primarily to the conduct of business, the command of a rabbinic authority of a non-Jewish, indigenous language is certainly a sign that the Bohemian Jews' cultural integration had taken root from the community's early beginnings.

The transition from the High Middle Ages to the Renaissance only reinforced the relatively secure position of Jews in Bohemia. Following the incorporation of Bohemia into the Habsburg Empire, the Jewish population of Prague doubled in less than two decades and new colonies started to spring up beyond the city's Jewish quarter. Prague became a celebrated center for Hebrew book production. Enjoying the protection of Emperors Maximilian II and Rudolph II during the late 16th and early 17th centuries, the Jews of Prague were allowed to engage in a variety of crafts, thereby curtailing the monopoly that the local Christian guilds had. The community's material prosperity led to the towering of Prague as a rabbinic center, epitomized in the figure of Rabbi Judah Löw ben Bezalel or the Maharal (1520-1609). The head of the celebrated Prague Yeshiva (rabbinic academy), the Maharal of Prague, is better known today by the fictional stories later circulated about him and about his brainchild, a supernatural creature called Golem that was made out of clay, designed to protect Prague's Jews.

During the 18th century, soon before the Age of Reason was about to dawn on Central Europe, Jewish life in Bohemia took a turn for the worse. Following the Thirty

Years' War (1618-1648), the Habsburg emperors sought to curb what they saw as the uncontrolled growth and expansion of Jewish communities. Against this background, Emperor Charles VI issued in 1726-1727 the infamous Familiants Laws, a repressive measure that

> *Jewish life in the Bohemian capital continued to flourish as the High Middle Ages wore on. Indeed, Prague is one of the only cities in Europe where one could find a continuous Jewish presence, stretching from the Middle Ages until the eve of the Holocaust...*

allowed only one son of each household to marry and establish himself on Bohemian soil. Rescinded more than a century later, following the 1848 revolution together with all other restrictions on the mobility of Jews, the measure did not achieve its intended goals. Taking advantage of the weakness of the Habsburg central government, many Jews who could not stay in Bohemia's urban centers chose instead to settle in the small towns and villages owned and run by the nobility. This by-product of the Familiants Laws had a significant impact on the future shape of the Bohemian Jewish community. The scattering of the Jews over almost 2,000 localities by the mid-19th century had made Bohemian Jewry far more fractured and weak. Yet it also exposed the recent Jewish arrivals to the countryside and to the language and culture of their new Gentile neighbors. From then on, a growing number of Jews would become Czech speakers and would play a significant role in the national revival of the Czech nation. Of the extended Strnad family, two members, Hedwig's mother, Eleonora Kohn, and Paul Strnad's father, were born precisely in such small Czech speaking localities whose Jewish population had been bolstered by the infamous Familiants Laws: in the small town of Božesov, and the larger market town of Nová Cerekev, both located south of Prague.

Jewish Bohemia, thus, became a land divided by the urban center of Prague versus the scattered Jewish community of the countryside. To this divide, another one would be added following one of the most significant events in the history of the community: the passing of a series of royal decrees in the early 1780s by the new Emperor Joseph II. Known as the Edict of Toleration, the most significant of this series of decrees – exemplary of the Age of Reason – was meant to "socially engineer" the Jews of the Habsburg Empire and turn them into what the new enlightened monarch saw as a more "productive" constituency. The attempt to turn the Jews away from their traditional occupations – that is, trade and money-lending – and turn them instead into a people of "productive" craftsmen and peasants had very little success. Yet, the introduction of mandatory Jewish elementary schools, where both religion and science were taught and where the language of instruction was now German, had a dramatic impact on the cultural shape of Bohemian Jewry. In the early 19th century, a growing number of Jews became German speakers. They took advantage of the greater professional liberties and the lifting of any restrictions on mobility in order to leave the Czech-speaking countryside and become a part of Bohemia's urban, German speaking elite. This was epitomized in the biographies of Paul and Hedwig, who, as the descendants of Jews arriving from the countryside, were born in two of Bohemia's urban centers toward the turn of the twentieth century: Hedwig in Prague, and Paul in the Sudetenland city of Ústí nad Laben, known as Aussig by German speakers.

The acculturation of Bohemian Jews in the course of the 19th century, accelerated in the early 20th century with a high intermarriage rate (between 1928-1933, 43.8% of the marriages in which one partner was Jewish were mixed). This high proportion, not surprisingly, was accompanied by the decline of Prague as a rabbinic center, apparent already in the early 19th century. It is noteworthy that the cultural and linguistic integration of Jews into the non-Jewish world surrounding them happened across Western and some parts of Eastern Europe. Yet, Bohemia might have arguably been the only place in Europe where this process of integration unfolded fairly peacefully and did not trigger the general public's discontent with Jewish integration, the backlash known as modern anti-Semitism.

It was the organic divide of Bohemia into a German and a Czech speaking community and, correspondingly, into two rival nationalist movements that accounts for the relative success of Bohemian Jewry's integration into the surrounding society. As the future of each of these movements seemed uncertain, both non-Jewish Germans and Czechs wished to enlist the Jews in their own camp. Rather than viewing the Jews as a foreign, undesirable element thrust between two powerful nationalist movements, the Jews of Bohemia, who often spoke both German and Czech, could act as a bridge between the two. In 1918, when the new republic of Czechoslovakia allowed Jews to declare themselves as a nationality, whether they spoke German or Czech, whether religiously observant or Zionist, approximately half did, showing a degree of comfort with their identity. The swiftness of the Nazi takeover of Czechoslovakia, the implementation of the equivalent of the Nuremberg Laws discriminating against Jews must have been utterly shocking to this well-integrated population.

Viewed from this perspective, it is easy to appreciate the desire of the Strnads to move to the United States, not only in order to save their own lives, but also to reach a new home where their interwar sense of a peaceful Jewish-Christian co-existence could be restored and where a multiplicity of cultures could thrive one alongside the other.

Sources:

Čapková, Kateřina. *Czechs, Germans, Jews? National Identity & the Jews of Bohemia.* New York and Oxford: Berghahn Books, 2012.

Kieval, Hillel. *Languages of Community, the Jewish Experience in the Czech Lands.* Berkeley: University of California Press, 2000.

Kieval, Hillel. "Bohemia and Moravia," The YIVO Encyclopedia of Jews in Eastern Europe. http://yivoencyclopedia.org/article.aspx/Bohemia_and_Moravia

Shay Pilnik is the Director of the Nathan and Esther Pelz Holocaust Education Resource Center in Milwaukee, Wisconsin. He has been an adjunct instructor at the University of Wisconsin-Milwaukee and the University of Wisconsin-Oshkosh, lecturing on a variety of topics including modern Jewish history, the Holocaust, and the religions of the world.

Jewish Museum Milwaukee

Moritz Strnad's department store in Aussig (Ústí nad Laben), Sudetenland, Bohemia

Modern Woman, Modern Czech, Modern Jew — Trapped

by Hasia Diner

The story of Hedwig Strnad, a fashion designer, her husband Paul, and their fruitless efforts to secure a visa to the United States after the face of the German occupation of Czechoslovakia offers both a dramatic tale of failed rescue and a highly visual way to tell it. Given the sketches she rendered in support of her pursuit of papers to enter the United States, her experiences should make for a superb and gripping museum exhibition.

There are several larger contexts that I would like to explore in these few pages to provide a humanities context for the Strnad exhibit.

Hedwig Strnad grew up in independent Czechoslovakia, a nation created out of the dismembered Austro-Hungarian Empire at the end of World War I. It promised much for Jews, particularly urban dwellers who partook of the cosmopolitan culture of what – unfortunately – became the interwar period as opposed to the post-World War I era. The newly created Czechoslovakia, led by Tomáš Masaryk, its first president, proclaimed the idea of religious and cultural pluralism. This rallying cry of the fledgling nation portended well for the Jews. The capital city, Prague, emerged as a hotbed of cultural ferment and modernism. It incubated Franz Kafka, for example, and although the writer achieved little fame in his lifetime, his writings can be seen as emblematic of a ferment in ideas that epitomized a rejection of the old world of the Emperor Franz Joseph, and its constraints which so many of the modernists saw as stuffy and tradition-bound. Elements within the city liberated themselves from the hierarchies and restrictions of the old Empire and many of its writers, artists, intellectuals, students, and young people embraced the culture of modernism that spread across Europe and America.

Hedwig Strnad's opportunity to participate in the fashion world can be seen as an example of the liberating atmosphere that pervaded the Prague of the new nation. The fashions she envisioned would have appealed to the "new woman," a figure whose emergence in the 1920s cut across national boundaries. Strnad's woman wore dresses with hemlines at or just below the knees. Her arms did not have to be encased in long sleeves, but showed themselves off, as simultaneously feminine and muscular, and her drawings depict slim, athletic looking women who looked forward, not feeling the need to be demure or hide their individuality. The woman whom Strnad imagined and dressed went out into the world. She wore suits for business and gowns for evening. No doubt she spent her leisure time in cafes, theaters, movie houses, and took to the thoroughfares ready to meet the world. In this decade, for example, women began to smoke in public, shedding inherited ideas

Factory workers in Prague after Nazi policies are enforced.

The Jewish Museum in Prague

about appropriate female behavior. She held her head at a cocky and self-confident angle as she turned her face directly to engage with onlookers. This woman envisioned by the Czech Strnad, no doubt based on those she had seen in the street, in shops, in places of entertainment, had her equivalents in the cities of Europe and America, produced by the end of the great ferment of the end of the nineteenth century and the upheavals that came with the "Great War."

As such, Strnad positioned herself as part of a new culture for women, one embodied in the kinds of dresses that she hoped to sew for them. Her drawings and her vision of women's bodies fit the age perfectly. As a Jewish woman, Strnad had clearly integrated modern emerging ideas about women and incorporated them into her own persona.

She and Paul represented the large numbers of highly modernized Jews of the interwar years who partook eagerly in the cultures of the places they lived, particularly when those societies had moved into the new century by rejecting the restrictions of the old. Urban Jews in particular, while retaining for the most part their affiliations as Jews, embraced new possibilities and liberated themselves from many of the internal Jewish communal restrictions which had previously set them apart from their non-Jewish neighbors. While many Jewish communal sources depict the Jews who perished in the Holocaust as traditional, as dwellers of traditional Jewish communities, the Strnads represent the vast number of Jews of Austria, Poland, Hungary, Czechoslovakia and elsewhere who enthusiastically embraced new opportunities. Even her drawings show a new kind of Jewish persona, of women unencumbered by traditional ideas of appropriate modesty, and the photograph of her and Paul make it clear that they had become thoroughly modern people.

That Strnad opted for work in and around the fashion industry made her utterly typical for European and American Jews of the early twentieth century, and indeed of before. The close association between Jews and garment making, at all levels of the field and in all branches, went back centuries, but by the nineteenth century the industrialization of the making of garments became a place where Jews congregated. They operated in this field from the bottom up and the top down. Jewish women and men did the sewing, whether at home, in sweatshops or in factories. Jewish men, in the main, operated those businesses and Jews in one city after another owned the shops where customers could buy the garments. Jews as designers, male and female, whether in London, Paris, New York, and in Strnad's case, Prague, left their mark on this field as well. Garment-making functioned as a crucial niche in the Jewish economy and became a pivotal place where they not only made money but helped change social norms of the societies in which they lived.

Jewish women in particular found the garment industry at its many rungs a particularly attractive way to make a living and to develop their individual talents. That a young Jewish woman like Hedwig Strnad saw her future in the designing of clothing should be hardly surprising or considered out of the ordinary. The production and marketing of dresses, blouses, hats, coats, and other apparel provided Jews with a world-wide livelihood and also with a powerful place from which to put their stamp on the larger culture.

Strnad's tragic fate lay in the hands of the Germans who marched into Czechoslovakia and destroyed the country's autonomy, as they imposed on its population their race-based policies against the Jews. Her disastrous outcome also lay in the hands of America's immigration policies, enacted in the 1920s, simultaneous with Czechoslovakia's emergence as an independent nation. Laws passed by Congress in 1921 and 1924 created the highly bureaucratized system based on national quotas. With these acts, the nation's long standing policy of numerically unrestricted European immigration came to an end, sealing the fate of Hedwig Strnad and the millions of other Jews of central and Eastern Europe, places which received relatively low quotas, making the prospect of securing a visa very difficult.

The Johnson-Reed Act of 1924 created a complex bureaucracy to manage the immigration system and put in place a complicated system by which individuals had to apply for visas to come as immigrants to the United States. They had to have an American sponsor and had to prove that they would not become public charges. Strnad, like so many other European Jews facing the Nazi menace, turned to their relatives in the United States to try to manipulate that system in order to help them get their visas. The number of visas barely met the press of applicants, who desperately wanted to leave Europe. Thousands upon thousands of American Jews, themselves of European origin, marshaled what resources they had to try to negotiate for their relatives who sought entry to America. Archives and records of Jewish organizations abound with letters of appeal to immigration officials written by American Jews on behalf of their relatives, trying to bring them to America. They contacted their congressmen hoping to circumvent the visa system.

The system however would not, and did not, budge. During the Depression, Americans as a whole resoundingly indicated in opinion polls that they did not want foreigners coming to America to take away the scant jobs available. They feared that a bad economy would only worsen with masses of immigrants. No doubt antipathy towards Jews played a role, although they had no more desire to take non-Jewish immigrants as Jews.

Alvin Strnad's efforts in behalf of his cousins resembled those undertaken by many American Jews. Their story remains to be told. Historians have depicted, inaccurately, American Jews as not terribly energetic in their rescue efforts for European Jewry on the eve of the Holocaust. That narrative does not in fact even fit the large Jewish organizations and the well-connected Jewish leaders who endeavored to help but could not get any results. And that narrative of inaction surely does not fit the American Jews who did what they could for their relatives.

From a letter Paul wrote to his brother-in-law. Hedy signed off with an added a message.

Hasia Diner, Ph.D., is the Professor of Hebrew and Judaic Studies and History, Paul S. and Sylvia Steinberg Professor of American Jewish History, and the Director, Goldstein-Goren Center for American Jewish History at New York University

What do Hedwig Strnad's Designs Reveal?

by Beverly Gordon

When Paul Strnad sent his wife's drawings to his cousin in Milwaukee, he was hoping an American dress manufacturer would find her flair for fashion compelling enough to provide an "affidavit of necessity" that would bring the couple to the United States. Hedwig's designs were upbeat and attractive, but not unique enough to warrant special treatment. Although we have little to go on with these eight images, we can nevertheless use them as a viewfinder to picture something of her life in Prague.

Hedwig was 40 years old in 1939, and it was only in her lifetime that Jews in her city had been able to become actual fashion "stars." Tailoring and dressmaking had long been understood in Eastern Europe as Jewish professions, with entire families commonly engaged in clothing production. Well into the 19th century, Jews were most associated with the mending and selling of secondhand clothes (this was possibly historically connected with the moneylending business, since pawned clothes had to be kept in good repair). Christian tailors' guilds tried to prohibit Jews from making new clothes, and their competition was significant enough to be one of the variables in the 1745 expulsion of the Jews from Prague. At least a fifth of the approximately 1400 families who returned three years later were involved with clothing, whether as tailors, button or trim makers, or merchants. Over time, as conditions changed (including the opening of the gates of the Prague ghetto in 1848), Jews became increasingly prominent in all aspects of the trade. Their entrepreneurship led to the rise of 19th century clothing factories, and by the end of that century, several Jewish families established couture houses that became vital parts of Prague society. Two of the most important were named for their founders, Hana Podolská and (Oldrich) Rosenbaum.

Such a (*haute*) *couture* (literally, "high style sewing") "house" was a business, with a head designer or *couturier*, who was usually the owner. He or she managed a team of designers, illustrators, cutters, tailors, and seamstresses, embroiderers, salespeople, and models. Many did extensive advertising and saw that their designs were regularly featured in fashion magazines. They focused on women's fashion. The Prague couture scene was lively and renowned. Couturiers regularly visited fashion shows in Paris and elsewhere, where they purchased the right to reproduce designs or made their own adaptions. They also brought back fine fabrics and trims. Prague couture was known for its precision, craftsmanship, and elegance; it was completely current with international style trends, but maintained its exquisite Czech tailoring and a unique local flavor. Couture garments were expensive, but by the interwar period, they were in high demand. The new nation of Czechoslovakia was forward-looking and modern.

As Jana Ulipová of Prague's Decorative Arts Museum explains it, the city's rapidly developing high society required clothing that expressed and symbolized its European ambitions.[1]

Couture was, of course, only for the wealthy. Less privileged women had their clothes made by independent dressmakers, who copied or adapted the styles set by couturiers. After World War I, ready-to-wear clothing was also increasingly available, although it was not yet as prevalent on the continent as in the United States.

Given this background, what are we to make of Hedwig Strnad's petition to come to Milwaukee as a dress designer? First, it is interesting that Alvin Strnad was approaching a dress *manufacturer* – i.e., a producer of ready-to-wear garments. We cannot be certain that Strnad was using the term accurately, or that the manufacturer was himself Jewish, but it is not unlikely. American Jews were important players in this industry in the 1930s. The center of production was in New York (Judith Weller's bronze statue of a yarmulke-bedecked garment worker now graces its historical "garment district"), but there were clothing production companies in the Midwest as well, including Jack Winter & Company and Rhea Manufacturing in Milwaukee. We don't know where Hedwig had been working, or in exactly what capacity, although Paul's letter implies that she was employed by someone else rather than operating independently. She might have worked in a small shop,

FIG 1. This fashion image from November, 1939 was the type made to illustrate patterns for the home sewer. Hedwig's sketches are similar.

FIGS 2 and 3: The hats depicted in these drawings, one on the cover of Germany's Mode und Heim (Fashion and Handwork) (December, 1939; see www.dideldum.gmxhome.de/heim.htm) and a sketch by Pearl Levy Alexander for André, September, 1939 are quite similar in style to those in Hedwig's renderings. Also note the red pocket handkerchief in the suit jacket on the right, which is visible in Hedwig's suit. The geometric designs on the fabrics, however, are not seen in her renderings.

or at one of the larger fashion houses.[2] We cannot be certain if she spent her time sketching designs that others would pattern out and sew (her drawings are competent and follow all the conventions of fashion illustration of the time), or worked in actual garment production (i.e., functioned as more of a dressmaker than a designer). She was certainly interested in keeping up with fashion trends; Paul's letter specifically requested that Alvin send a fashion journal since they were unavailable to Hedwig and she wanted to be informed about the new Paris styles. We must look to the sketches themselves to assess Hedwig's relationship to fashion.

The images sent to America were in keeping with mainstream women's fashion. They did not depict unusual or memorable women; rather, the models were bland, generic stereotypes that represented a kind of every woman ideal. The garments were not that memorable either. Unlike the daring contemporary designs of more *avant garde* couturiers like Elsa Schiaparelli, who played with shape, reference and material, Hedwig's outfits were flattering and for the most part up-to-date with current trends, but they echoed rather than led the kind of illustrations one would find in a fashion magazine. Her sketches include minor outdated elements. Her apparent predilection for floral prints, for example, did not match the emphasis on geometrics that dominated the style centers. Her high, round necklines were also not typical in 1939. These details may have reflected the fact that Hedwig had no access to up-to-the minute imagery, or perhaps represented local preference or personal taste. The one (undated) picture we have of Hedwig shows her wearing a garment with a similar round neck.

My hunch is that Hedwig worked for a smaller or less fashion-forward shop. I believe she was quite used to

making drawings of this kind, since she had mastered the conventional look and pose of the mannequin. Her figures are anonymous and without personality. They do not look directly at the viewer, and they stand in a narrow range of stylized postures—with one hand bent at an angle and the other straight down, or with two hands clasped out in front. Their bodies are mere scaffolds, if you will, for the clothes they wear, and because they are rendered in simple outline form, they look much like paper dolls. The sketches, and indeed the poses themselves, also recall the kind of fashion drawings produced by pattern companies (see Figure 1) who provided generic images to highlight the "smartness" their products afforded. (In America, for example, images like this appeared monthly in *The Delineator* magazine.[3]) Hedwig's sketches also show a familiarity with fabrics and the way they would hang, fit, drape or hug the body. The suits and coat dress [4, 8, 5] would have been made with wool, and the renderings show them skimming the body differently than the cloth in the day dresses (1, 3; cotton or rayon) or evening gown (6; silk or rayon). Finally, the clothes look simple enough to be made in

FIG 4. Hedwig's long gown was probably conceived of as a satin underdress covered by a sheer silk cloth. Such styles were considered very romantic, suitable for dancing (think of Ginger Rogers), and contrasted strongly with the more militaristic-looking business suits. This one by Harvey Nichols & Co. was featured in 1937 in Vogue. Hedwig's design features pinned-on artificial flowers, perhaps of the type that she and Paul were constructing when they could no longer keep their jobs.

quantity, meaning Hedwig could have been designing for a ready-to-wear market.

What do the fashion images tell us about the iconic European woman in 1939? She was young, slim, and small-waisted. She was modest, but not retiring; she was someone who regularly appeared in public, showing her face and legs, and wearing makeup. Some of the time she reflected the efficiency of the workplace – her suits had detailing familiar from menswear and military uniforms – but even when she was dressed more play-fully, her broad, emphasized shoulders evoked strength and a kind of manly confidence.[4] This woman did not have to do physical labor (there are no work clothes or practical shoes, and she wears dainty gloves). She did however labor at her appearance, taking time to roll or perm her hair into a neat, face-framing style and apply lipstick and rouge; and she cared about having the right outfit for the occasion, and the right, well-coordinated accessories. She had leeway in her choice of hat, but she always wore it at the proper angle. She was "modern" and independent, in other words, and did not broadcast religious or ethnic difference, but she conformed to conventions and sartorial rules.

Hedwig's designs show her to be a woman assimilated into international cosmopolitan style, who was producing designs for society women and actresses, some of whom may have been equally assimilated themselves. It is amazing to realize that it had only been a century since Prague Jews had been confined to the ghetto. Ironically, after the Holocaust when the city was emptied of most Jews – its skilled fashion work force – Prague had trouble rebounding as a fashion center. The final death blow was brought by the Soviet takeover in 1948, after which private companies, including fashion houses, were converted to cooperatives and state enterprises.

References

Knox, Kathleen. "Fa-Fa-Fa-Fa-Fashion: Turn to the West," The Prague Post. Posted: June 29, 1994. www.praguepost.com/archivescontent/15241-fa-fa-fa-fa-fashion-turn-to-the-west.html, accessed August 16, 2013.

Meyer, Jacey. "A Night out in Prague, in the Early 20th Century," CzechPosition.com, October 1, 2012, www.ceskapozice.cz/en/czech-living/arts-leisure/night-out-prague-early-20th-century, accessed August 16, 2013.

Uchalová, Eva, Zora Damová, and Viktor Šlajchrt. Prague Fashion Houses 1900—1948. Prague: Museum of Decorative Arts with Arborvitae Press, 2011.

Henry Wasserman, "Tailoring," Jewish Virtual Library, www.jewishvirtuallibrary.org/jsource/judaica/ejud_0002_0019_0_19521.html, accessed August 16, 2013.

[1] Jana Ulipová cited in Jacey Meyer, "A Night out in Prague, in the Early 20th Century."

[2] A 1920s-era evening or party dress by František Strnad is featured in Jacey Meyer, "A Night Out in Prague, in the Early 20th Century," but it is not clear what fashion house it was associated with. I have been unable to ascertain if this designer is any relation to Hedwig, but in this context the fact that so many of the couture houses and other clothing businesses were family affairs is intriguing. In either case the strong reputation of Prague fashion might have given her the confidence to request a designer position in America.

[3] This was published by the Butterick pattern company.

[4] In 1933, The Delineator referred to some of the shoulder treatments as "stickups." They were clearly meant to draw attention to themselves and give the woman more presence.

Beverly Gordon, Ph.D., is a Professor Emerita (retired), Design Studies Department, School of Human Ecology and Previous Faculty Associate, Folklore, Gender and Women's Studies Programs, College of Letters & Science, at the University of Wisconsin, Madison.

FIG 5. Hedwig's original illustrations

What's in a Sketch? Fashion, Women, and Jewish Contributions to the Garment Industry

by Sara Hume

The words, images and designs of Paul and Hedwig Strnad, provide a glimpse into a life of a family that is strikingly relatable and familiar. The letter and drawings attest to the intelligence, talent and skill that was lost with their deaths. The tragedy of their deaths was obviously compounded by the fact that they were just one among millions of families to die. The designs by Hedwig that Paul mailed to the United States are precious testimony to the flourishing fashion industry in Prague in the early twentieth century, an industry that was irrevocably depleted by the Holocaust.

The discordance between these designs and the tragic circumstances behind their creation is striking. The drawings were not created as a form of personal expression, but were rather a product created for a professional purpose, and as such, they conceal rather than reveal insights into Hedwig's situation. Paul Strnad mailed these designs to the United States to prove Hedwig's competence as a designer. Perhaps she sought to cater directly to her understanding of what American women wanted to wear, but they nevertheless suggest the extent to which the fashion industry in Prague was closely aligned with mainstream Western fashion. The designs are noteworthy not for their brilliance and innovation, but for their very ordinariness. The bright palate she favored for these designs, for instance, was consistent with the colors in the Sears Catalogue from Fall/Winter 1939-40, which forecasted "a colorful season."[1] Because of the predominance of black and white images from this period it is easy to assume the colors were dull and drab. The bright blues, purples and reds evoke the Technicolor optimism of the film adaptation of *The Wizard of Oz* more than the horror of Nazi-occupied Czechoslovakia. The styles of the late 1930s foreshadowed many of the characteristics of the 1940s – the broad shoulders, knee-length skirts, the crisp suits. The prescience that Hedwig's designs demonstrate is particularly haunting considering that she would not live to see the styles her work presaged.

Hedwig's designs were the height of fashion for 1939 and lack obvious clues that identify them as coming from Prague. This absence of regional distinction is a testament to the homogenization of Western fashion that prevailed by the early 20th century. By that time, Prague had a thriving fashion industry that worked to validate itself by promoting connections to the French fashion industry. Even when seeking a future in the

Jewish Museum Milwaukee Collection

American fashion industry, Hedwig wished for fashion magazines from Paris. Prague fashion houses would send representatives to Paris, and French designers were welcomed to Prague where they were invited to put on fashion shows.[2] Developing links to French culture was appealing to the burgeoning country of Czechoslovakia. The selection of Paris as a model for the Prague fashion industry was in a sense a rejection of Berlin. The prestige of Paris largely depended on its cultivation of high-end fashion. Berlin's fashion industry took a different tack with the proliferation of lower end fashion production. Berlin was a large center for the production of ready-to-wear, or Konfektion, which was

---

1 Sears, Roebuck and Co. Sears Catalogue, Fall/Winter 1939-40, p. 97.
2 Eva Uchalová, Prazské módní salony – Prague Fashion Houses, 1900-1948 (Umeleckoprumyslové museum v Praze; Arbor vitae, 2011), 71.

sold across Europe, even in France. The simplification of women's wear, which had started in the early 20th century, facilitated the production of ready-to-wear clothing. The inherent anonymity of workers in the Berlin ready-to-wear industry contrasted with the fame and celebrity of French haute couture houses. However, the ultimate reason the reputation of Berlin does not compare to that of Paris as a center of fashion production was the destruction wrought by the Holocaust. The extermination of the Jewish population across Central Europe disrupted the development of this critical industry and shifted the center of ready-to-wear production to America. The Strnads sought fashion news from Paris but they pinned their hope of a future in the fashion industry in America.

The development of the fashion industry, including both the system of production and the demographics, followed a similar course throughout Western Europe in general and Central Europe more specifically, until World War II. Hedwig was typical of the workers in the industry in that she was female and Jewish. Rather than a model of industrialization centered on factory production, the clothing industry depended on piecework performed by workers – primarily female – who worked in their own homes. The work was not steady, but served to supplement the family income, particularly in difficult times. While it is unclear from the materials on the Strnads whether Hedwig had worked from home or owned her own shop, it is clear that by 1939 the family depended on the money she could earn out of the house. Paul wrote that he was helping Hedwig make artificial flowers. Such work was typical of the sort of piecework done by women home workers. The system of home work had served to marginalize female workers, in part because the isolation of the workers outside of a shared workplace limited their visibility and prevented their organization. However, when Jews were forced out of their jobs during the Nazi's program of Aryanization, the flexibility and invisibility of home work proved a benefit. This sort of work had never been adequate to support a family and was not for the Strnads, but it remained the last means of support in a period of desperation.

Clothing is a fundamental means of identifying oneself and marking differences between groups, yet in the case of the Jews of Prague, clothing was a means of integrating themselves into society. The fashionable and smart clothes worn by the Strnads in the photograph sent to Milwaukee do not identify them as Jewish or as Czech. The participation of Jews in clothing production helped contribute to their assimilation into Prague culture.

Jewish Museum Milwaukee Collection

Both Christian and Jewish residents of Prague would have bought their clothes from Jewish dressmakers, tailors, and shop owners. In a sense, the Jews dressed themselves in the same style as they dressed gentiles. Dressing in the same way as Christians, obviously was inconsistent with adherence to Jewish dress traditions. Both Hedwig's and Paul's heads are uncovered. She wears neither a cap nor a wig while he doesn't wear a yarmulke and is clean-shaven. The adoption of fashionable Western dress was consistent with the generally non-observant character of Jewish life in Prague.

While clothing distinctions between Christians and Jews in Prague were often negligible, the distinctions in dress between residents of Prague on the one hand and residents of the rest of the Czech lands were more pronounced. The preservation of distinctive dress practices by rural Jews was more widespread, but so was the development of distinctive dress among non-Jewish Bohemians and Moravians. Like linguistic choices, clothing practices became a clear means of communicating identity in a region with a number of possible cultural affiliations. However, while Jews readily adopted either the German or the Czech language as they assimilated into Czech society, they were shut out of the traditional dress practices. The possibility of assimilation in Prague was greatly facilitated by the system of modern dress, a system to which Jews were allowed equal access. Fashionable dress appears to have been the normative choice, but in fact, across the Czech lands a number of different choices were available. The environment created by Jewish cultural specificity was in fact, remarkable.

The letter, with its accompanying designs and photograph that Paul mailed to his cousins in Milwaukee, provides a small but telling window into the lives of Jews in Prague on the eve of World War II. They attest to the dynamism of the Prague fashion industry before the Holocaust. The modern fashion system that had emerged by the end of the beginning of the twentieth century provided employment for thousands of Jews both in Prague and throughout Central Europe, but it also provided a means of assimilating into European society. In contrast to traditional forms of dress that highlighted local differences and made sharp distinctions according to religion, the homogenization of Western dress by the early twentieth century facilitated assimilation and integration. Sadly this glimpse into Jewish life in Prague is just one more piece of evidence of the immeasurable loss and tremendous waste of the Holocaust.

3 Franzoi, *At the Very Least She Pays the Rent: Women and German Industrialization*, 1871-1914 (Westport, Conn.: Greenwood Press, 1985).

Sara Hume, Ph.D. is the Assistant Curator and Assistant Professor at the Kent State University Museum.

The Destruction of Bohemian Jewry

by Jane A. Avner

The year is 1938. Czechoslovakia, which consists of Bohemia, Moravia, Slovakia and Subcarpathian Ruthenia, is the only functioning democracy in Central and Eastern Europe. Minority populations, including Jews, have full and equal rights. World War II will not begin until September 1, 1939 when Germany invades Poland, but the impact of the expansionist goals of the Nazis is apparent to the fledgling democracy, only formed in 1918.

In September, 1938, leaders from France, Great Britain, Italy, and Germany met in Munich and, in violation of previous treaties, agreed that a portion of Czechoslovakia, the Sudetenland, would be ceded to Nazi Germany. The Sudetenland was a narrow, crescent-shaped area of mostly German-speaking Czech citizens on its eastern border with Germany, Austria and Poland. The following month, the German army occupied this territory. Many of its 25,000 Jews, reacting to intensifying German anti-Semitism already in evidence in their home towns, headed to the south, mostly to Prague. These refugees joined other German-speaking Jews from Austria and Germany who fled to Prague and surrounding areas after the Nazis rose to power in 1933. By March 1939 the Nazi conquest of Czechoslovakia was complete. The promising democratic republic no longer existed; the four-province confederation broke down. Slovakia pulled away, aligning with the Nazis and the Carpathian area was ceded to Hungary. Bohemia (where Prague was located) and Moravia were absorbed into Germany and became known as the "Protectorate."

After the occupation, Jews were subjected to laws similar to the Nuremberg Laws in Germany, including the seizure of property and businesses; exclusion of Jewish children from non-Jewish schools and adults from their previous professions; mandatory wearing of a yellow Star of David; and abolition of many other human rights.

The Prague Jewish community was led by the Central Office for Jewish Immigration. František Weidmann and Jakob Edelstein worked to facilitate immigration and ameliorate poor living conditions. At least 26,000 were successful in immigrating to Palestine, South America, and Western Europe before those avenues of escape were closed. Edelstein became aware of Nazi plans to deport Jews to the east and was determined that Czech Jews be spared this fate. To that aim, he and Weidmann worked with the Nazis to establish what they thought would be a productive labor camp in the town of Terezín which would safeguard the approximately 92,000 Jews remaining in the Protectorate.

The leaders of the Nazi occupation in Prague, Reinhard Heydrich, and later, Adolf Eichmann, had very different goals for the camp better known as Theresienstadt. The

Anti-Jewish Campaign Sweeps Over Territory In Reich "Protectorate"

Borders Closed As German Troops March Into Czecho-Slovakia; Further Restrictions Imminent

ARRESTS AND SUICIDES MOUNT

Prague—(JTA)— The anti-Jewish campaign in German-occupied parts of former Czecho-Slovakia gained momentum this week, to the accompaniment of increasing arrests and suicides. Escape by emigration was prevented as German troops closed the borders, as was done in Austria a year ago. Various reports told of border riots as Jews and others sought to escape, the halting of 300 Jews at Maerisch-Ostrau and 100 at Lobositz, and the detention of 200 Jews who sought to emigrate to San Domingo with an equal number of poorer Jews.

Jewish suicides were said to be reaching great proportions, but no figures were available. Four Jews in one house were reported to have killed themselves by leaping from the window. Newspapers reported 20 suicides of Jews a day. The ousting of Jews from the country's economic life went forward rapidly. Jewish physicians and lawyers were forbidden to practice. The Prague Merchant's association expelled all Jewish members, their shops already taken over by Nazi commissars. It was announced that all Jewish employes in the film industry had "resigned."

Arrests of Jews and anti-Nazis were estimated at various figures, the highest being 12,000 as Nazis searched Jewish homes for "Communist arms caches." In Slovakia, Hlinka guards confiscated Jewish money and valuables and took over Jewish owned automobiles and trucks. In Bratislava, sentries were posted in front of apartment houses to prevent Jews from leaving with parcels. The few Bratislava Jews permitted to cross the Danube into Hungary were allowed to take only 500 crowns ($17).

Jewish relief work in Prague was halted by seizure of the Jewish community's funds. The office of the

HIAS - ICA Emigration association was among Jewish organizations and institutions closed down. Panic-stricken Jews were hiding or making frantic efforts to emigrate. Hundreds gathered outside the British consulate in Prague, shouting, "We want to get away!"

Extension of the Nuremberg laws was indicated in Chancellor Hitler's decree formally announcing incorporation of Bohemia and Moravia as a "protectorate" in the German reich. The decree, broadcast by German foreign minister Joachim von Ribbentrop, said that "German-blooded residents of the protectorate will become German citizens subject to the laws protecting German blood and German honor."

A transport of 160 Jews en route to Palestine got across the frontier shortly before the Germans occupied Prague. The transport included the famous poet, Max Brod; the journalist, Dr. Felix Weltsch and a number of other prominent Zionists. All held Palestine immigration certificates in the capitalist category. Meanwhile, many Jews have fled from Bohemia-Moravia to Slovakia, hoping for better treatment there because Slovakian Jews had been among the supporters of Dr. Josef Tiso, premier of the new Nazi protectorate.

Payment was stopped on all Jewish accounts in Prague banks. Bruenn's largest synagogue was destroyed by a fire assumed to be incendiary.

Welfare, Refugee Agencies Collapse

Prague—(WNS)— The efforts of social welfare agencies with British and American cooperation to aid political refugees and Jews to get out of the country collapsed with the arrest of at least forty-seven of their [Continued on Page 3]

Wisconsin Jewish Chronicle March 24, 1939

Nazis always intended it to be a transit camp for sending its prisoners to ghettos and death camps in Eastern Europe. Beginning in late 1941, approximately 74,000

Czech Jews would be transported from the Protectorate to Theresienstadt, and of those, 80% would be deported to an assortment of ghettos and concentration camps – ultimately to their death.

Several factors have given Theresienstadt a reputation of being a "model" concentration camp. In truth, conditions in Theresienstadt were deplorable. Disease, malnutrition, and overcrowding were commonplace. In addition to the Czech Jews (many of whom who were secular, Zionists, and active in the arts and sciences) the Nazis sent prominent people from Western Europe that they dared not execute outright; thus, there was a collection of well-known and talented individuals from all over Europe, including academics, rabbis, composers, and artists, who organized social and educational programming. In mid-1944, instigated by the presence of Danish prisoners, Red Cross representatives from Sweden and Denmark insisted on inspecting Theresienstadt. The Germans cleaned up the camp for the Red Cross and filmed the visit as a propaganda exercise. They subsequently sent all the presentation participants to Auschwitz where they perished.

By war's end, 152,000 Jews from 16 countries spent time in Theresienstadt; 34,000 died in the camp, 87,000 were deported and murdered in other camps or ghettos, and 30,000 survived.

The Strnad family was particularly devastated. Of the individuals we have identified, all Jewish members but two were sent to Theresienstadt. The two exceptions were Brigitte and Liselotte Neumann (Hedwig and Paul's nieces, ages 9 and 12 in 1939) who went to England on a *Kindertransport* [a children's rescue mission] where both survived the war. Of the sixteen who were in

Theresiendstadt, three survived: Hedwig's sister Margareta, her husband Arnold and their daughter Eva.

The rest of the family perished because they were then sent to other locations. Paul, Hedwig, and Hedwig's mother were deported to Warsaw. Most Warsaw Ghetto residents died of malnutrition or disease in the ghetto or were further deported to Treblinka between July and November, 1942. Paul's father Moritz and sister Martha (with her husband Richard and daughter Charlota) were sent from Theresienstadt to Treblinka concentration camp, near Warsaw; Paul's sister Hilde died in Riga, Latvia; another sister, Ernestine, died in Trawniki, a forced labor camp twenty miles from Lublin, Poland; Hedwig's sister Gertrud, brother-in-law Vilem, and 8-year-old nephew Petr-André died in Maly Trostinets, near Minsk, Poland; Helene (Brigitte and Liselotte's mother) died in Auschwitz, Poland; their father, Dr. Ernst Neumann, was not Jewish, but was known to be an anti-Nazi, and he too spent time in labor camps. He survived the war.

Tragically, the Strnads serve as a perfect example of the destruction of the vibrant community of Bohemian Jews. Over 80% of their family died. Similarly, over 80% of Czech Jewry perished during the Holocaust.

Sources
Brod, Petr, apková, Kate ina, and Frankl, Michal. www.yivoencyclopedia.org/article.aspx/Czechoslovakia, 2010.

Rothkirchen, Livia. *The Jews of Bohemia and Moravia Facing the Holocaust.* Lincoln: University of Nebraska Press, 2005.

Jane A. Avner, Ph.D., is an Historical Researcher for the Jewish Museum Milwaukee and a Community Study Consultant at the Milwaukee Jewish Federation.

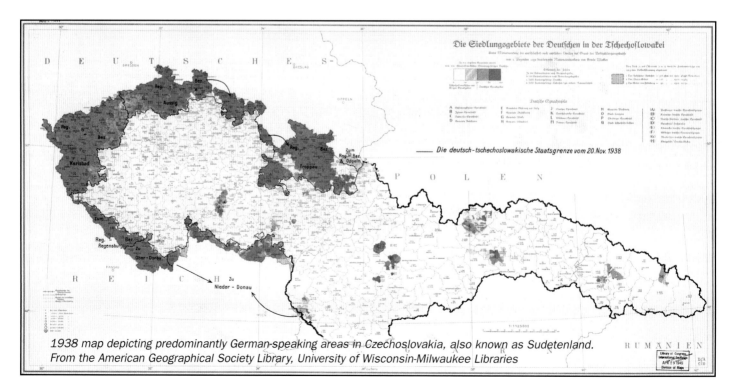

1938 map depicting predominantly German-speaking areas in Czechoslovakia, also known as Sudetenland. From the American Geographical Society Library, University of Wisconsin-Milwaukee Libraries

The Story Continues: Hedwig's Niece Stitches Together More Pieces

by Tyler D. Grasee

Without the contribution of eyewitnesses, people think of history as an uninvolving set of dates, faceless names, and numbers. While it is possible to reconstruct the past without eyewitnesses, there is something invaluable about making a human connection. It is important not only to "know the facts," but also to envision them through the eyes of an individual who can relate human emotion and details that could be misinterpreted or even lost entirely.

Jewish Museum Milwaukee

Brigitte Neumann Rohaczek at her oral history interview in February, 2014.

In February, 2014, I interviewed a survivor of the Holocaust and niece of Hedwig Strnad, Brigitte Rohaczek. My interview was crucial to the advancement of this exhibit and it deepened our understanding of the Holocaust, of tolerance, and of how much was lost.

This exhibit was developed with limited primary resources: a letter to Alvin Strnad, eight dresses, and one picture. This letter was all that told Hedwig's story and it would inspire readers and provide a basis for further exploration. Significant details were collected from personal testimonials from Yad Vashem's Central Database of Shoah Victim's Names housed in Israel. These testimonials were submitted by a woman named Brigitte Neumann Rohaczek. Upon providing descriptions of the transports and subsequent deaths of her relatives, Brigitte listed herself as Hedwig Strnad's niece living in Germany. The staff of the Jewish Museum Milwaukee tried to locate Brigitte based upon the information she submitted, but all attempts failed. Both the Museum associates and I agreed that it was an astonishing coincidence, possibly even fate, that I was living in Berlin, Germany as a student at the time the exhibit was being developed. Like others who had learned about Hedwig, I was absolutely enthralled by her story and felt the need to discover more. Through an internet search and my ability to speak German, I found Brigitte on a list of individuals who provided eyewitness testimony for Dr. Iris Guske's book, *Trauma and Attachment in the Kindertransport Context: German-Jewish Child Refugees' Accounts of Displacement and Acculturation in Britain*. The title of this book gave significant hints to the details of Brigitte's survival. With the help of Dr. Guske, who works at a language institute in Kempten, Germany, contact was established with Brigitte. While preparing to interview Brigitte in Nuremberg

on behalf of the Jewish Museum Milwaukee, I envisioned the surprise and intrigue she would express in learning about her distant relatives in America and the interest in developing an exhibit about her aunt.

The importance of this interview was clear from the moment Brigitte began to speak of her childhood, specifically of her aunt. Though Brigitte was not at all surprised that a foreign museum was developing an exhibit on her family, she was surprised that the focus wasn't on other prominent members of her family, like an uncle who was nominated for a Nobel Prize in Medicine. Based on Brigitte's reaction, it was clear to me that she came from a highly successful family. As we began the interview, she immediately referenced *TanteHedy* ["Auntie Hedy"] or *Hedwig*. Until this point, Museum professionals referred to her as *Hedvika*, the Czech equivalent of Hedwig, as it appears in the Holocaust citation indexing, including records from Theresienstadt and Yad Vashem. In reality, Brigitte and Hedwig's family was comprised of Czech Jews who identified culturally as German. German was their native language and they identified strongly with German *Hochkultur* ["High culture"], and certainly did not refer to themselves with the Czech equivalents of their names (i.e. *Hedvika* for *Hedwig* or *Pavel* for *Paul*). This discovery was crucial in understanding Hedwig Strnad, her family, and her background. Regardless of intention, it would have been an unfortunate choice to represent the fashion designer's life in a way which would have been foreign to her. We could not refer to her using a name that was not her own and which was, moreover, exclusively used in the records of her murder.

Brigitte also casually mentioned her Aunt Hedwig's red

NATHAN	Susanne	4649	26.10.26	with guarantor	As above		As above
METTEL	Helga	5639	21. 2.27	c/o Mrs F Richardson, 167 Welford Road, Northampton.	R. A. Overton, Rugby Committee, The Green, Bilton, Rugby.	Czech Section	
METTEL	Susanne	8183	24. 1.25	c/o Mr.T.T.Richardson 72 Windsor Crescent, Northampton.	As above	Czech Section	
NEUMANN	Brigitte	5871	17. 3.30	c/o Mrs. Williams, Dunromin, Gobowen, Salop.	Thos. P. Craigside, Pant, Oswestry, Salop.	Czech Section	
NEUMANN	Liselotte	5870	18.12.27	as above	as above	Czech Section	
NEUMANN	Edith	4695	30.12.27	c/o guarantor c/o Mrs Bigwood for Hitherham G.	Heightley, Park Drive, Oswestry, Salop.		Guarantee arranged before re-em.gut was requisite.
NEUMANN	Melitta	4694	27. 6.30	c/o guarantor	Mrs Borden for W.Co. as above		as above
NEUMANN	Jan	12611	26. 6.24	c/o Mary Wragg 21 Hansford Avenue, Manchester 19. 132, Wigan Rd, Brans Head, Wigan.	Rev. E. H. Lee, 18 Devreux Court, Strand, W.C.2.	Personal guarantee	
NEUMANN	Kaethe	7381	8. 7.22	c/o Mrs. Hobart-Hampden Movement 55 Fitzroy Road, N.W.1.	Movement	Movement	?
NEUSTADT	Liesl	7097	30. 4.34	with guarantor	Jas. Priestley Price, 77 Carmarthen Ave., East Cosham, Hants.	Czech Section	
NOHEL	Eva Inez	5032	25.10.30	with guarantor The Herbat Arms, Kerry, nr. Newtown, Wales.	Otto Kahn, 11 Handel Close, Edgware Road, Maddan, Edgware.	Personal guarantee	Eugen & Eva Nohel C.T.
NOVAK	Sonja	8587	3. 9.24	c/o Mrs. Pl Hall,	Mrs. D. A. Stone,	Bank guarantee	

Brigitte and sister Liselotte Kindertransport record.

---

hair. The vividness of this image was indescribable as I paired physical description with anecdotes about Hedwig's refined, dignified personality, all while glancing at photographs of Hedwig with her own niece. "She was red-haired…and always very nicely-dressed. And she was very fashionable; she smoked. And they were always in a good mood, these people. They had a lovely life. They were kind. They were content." Through this experience, guided by Mrs. Rohaczek, Hedwig Strnad became more than a concept, one of countless victims of the Holocaust. It humanized her story and forced me to face exactly how much was lost in one of the darkest segments of human history: how many individuals like Hedwig will be remembered incorrectly, simply as a statistic, a name on a list, or totally unremembered?

The story of the Strnad family deserves our special attention, not only because of its connection to the United States, but also because it is atypical of most stories of the Holocaust that are showcased. This story focuses not on the lives of well-known individuals – men with political ideologies, or scientists – this story focuses on the lives of virtually unknown yet incredible and inspiring people. While this exhibit discusses the lives of a single family, Hedwig Strnad reminds us of the incredible amount of talent lost in the Holocaust; in this sense, she and her family are symbolic of the struggles of countless others. In Paul's letters to his cousin Alvin in Milwaukee, he attempts to arrange safe passage for himself and his wife from Czechoslovakia to the United States in the wake of Nazi terror. Paul attempts to demonstrate his family's financial independence; he cites not his own professional abilities, but rather the fashion expertise of his wife. Paul sends Hedwig's sketches, from which the exhibit would later grow. In her interview, Brigitte juxtaposes her jolly, good-natured aunt with Hedy the businesswoman. "The whole Strnad family was a very happy family and very kind…Auntie Hedwig had a sort of big room where there were sewing machines, and where they were sewing clothes; and the girls that were employed there used to sew little dresses for my dolls." The occupation of seamstress was one of the most common amongst European Jewish women at this time; Hedwig's life as a professional and a

businesswoman in the public eye had become fully accepted in Prague society after World War I.

Both Brigitte Rohaczek and Hedwig Strnad witnessed an unusual number of changes in their nation's government, which drastically altered their lives. They were born as citizens of the Austro-Hungarian Empire and were members of a very traditional, patriarchal society. The establishment of a democratic republic of Czechoslovakia marked their subsequent sociocultural liberation, including the governmental recognition of the Jews of Czechoslovakia as full citizens with equal civil rights. A mere 20 years later, with the annexation of the Sudetenland, a significant portion of western Czechoslovakia encompassing large portions of German-speaking Bohemia (Brigitte and Hedwig's homeland), they lost these rights, in addition to their general social acceptance. This applied not only to Jews living within Czechoslovakian borders, but to all minorities deemed "inferior" by Nazi pseudo-science including the Sinti and Roma and members of ethnic groups not considered to be related to the "German race."

Brigitte Rohaczek's interview on the life of Hedwig Strnad reminds us why learning about history is so important; history is a living entity, full of variation, multiple perspectives, and hard-learned lessons. Brigitte's perspectives on her Aunt Hedwig, including the descriptions of her sense of fashion, jolly disposition, and dark red hair breathe life into this family's story and provide details that would have been unknown. Brigitte furthermore describes how she survived the Holocaust before other members of her family were murdered. "They organized, first in Germany, these transports for children, and then they went to Czechoslovakia…and we were the last one to go. And the one that was still arranged to go after us could not go, because in-between was the war." Thanks to the organization of a relative and the generosity of British benefactors, Brigitte escaped to England with thousands of other Czechoslovakian children in the Kindertransport. Brigitte survived, while the majority of her family did not. This shows the tragic loss of voices in the Holocaust and the importance of this interview. Thanks to her astonishing memory, we are closer to understanding Hedwig and the Strnad family. The great changes these women faced during their lifetimes, the survival of Brigitte as a refugee, and the murder of Hedwig all attest to the fleeting nature of freedom and the necessity for us to become active participants in determining our own.

Tyler D. Grasee is a student at Lawrence University in Appleton, Wisconsin and a former intern at the Jewish Museum Berlin. His academic interests include Jewish history in the German-speaking world and German language.

A Letter from Karen Strnad to Her Cousins Brigitte and Liesl

July 4, 2014

Dearest Brigitte and Liesl,

I am your American cousin, Karen Strnad. We share the same Great (Great) Grandparents, Marie and Abraham Strnad. Marie and Abraham had four sons, including your Grandfather Moritz and my Great Grandfather Benedict. Benedict immigrated to the United States.

We would have known each other had the Holocaust never happened. Or, we would have known each other had your Grandfather Moritz emigrated from Bohemia with my Great Grandfather Benedict in 1891, or at any time before immigration restrictions in the U.S. and the Nazi conquest of Europe closed the gates of life to our Bohemian family.

An absolutely unbelievable sequence of events has brought us together. The story starts in the 1800's and is a long one which I would like to share with you, and that I would like for you to share with me. It is a story that exemplifies how history is ongoing, and what a profound effect a museum can have on our lives. It is a story of four generations of family members' ongoing efforts over three centuries to stay connected and their desperate, coordinated fight for survival. It is the ultimate love story - how Paul Strnad's letters pin his and his wife's survival on his wife's talents, paramount to his own. It is a tragedy. It is a story still in the making.

In 1938 and 1939 my Grandfather Alvin received letters from your Uncle Paul Strnad. The letters included family photographs and a series of dress designs by his wife Hedy that he hoped might lead to a job, a sponsor and a visa. Benedict, Alvin and his sister Mildred tried desperately to get him and Hedy out of Bohemia – to no avail.

My father Burton found the letters after my Grandfather Alvin died, and donated the letters, photographs and dress designs to the Milwaukee Jewish Archives. The Jewish Museum Milwaukee has conducted extensive research about our family and has created actual dresses from Hedy's original designs. The Jewish Museum Milwaukee exhibit provides a unique window into the history, not only of our family, but of the entire Jewish people. It is our shared story and a story to the world about loss, and that there should never be another Holocaust.

We did not know you were alive until now. I understand that you did not know we were alive either. It was because of your submitting our ancestors' Pages of Testimony to Yad Vashem, Israel's Holocaust Museum in Jerusalem, that the researchers from the Jewish Museum Milwaukee discovered that you and your sister survived by leaving on one of the last Kindertransports that left Prague in 1939.

In the letters we have from your Uncle Paul Strnad to my Grandfather Alvin Strnad, amidst the atrocities in which he was living, Paul mentioned sending stamps as a very thoughtful gift from the Old Country to the New. I too would like to send you stamps in honor of our ancestors' tradition.

Please find attached some family pictures and the letter from your Uncle Paul to my Grandfather Alvin which ultimately led to our being reunited. Also included are sketches of your Aunt Hedy's dresses and a copy of the page of the Kindertransport registration book with your name on it that allowed you to get on the train.

This is for starters. I have much more to share with you.

Most importantly, on behalf of the entire Strnad family, with the sincerest of emotion, I want you to know... we love you.

Just before my Great Grandfather Benedict died in 1939, he wrote the family a letter telling the history of the Strnad family, about him, and what he wished for our lives. I would like to reiterate what he said: "It is my wish that you have a family gathering whenever possible. May you live in the best of health, happiness and peace." After seventy five years, "whenever" is finally here. I am so excited to meet you.

I will close this letter with the same closing my Great Grandfather Benedict used...

With eternal love,

Karen Strnad

The Creation of "Hedy's Line"

by Ellie Gettinger

Hedy (signature)

The eight dress designs created by Hedwig Strnad were given to the Milwaukee Jewish Archives in 1997, more than ten years before the Jewish Museum Milwaukee opened. When they were received, director Kathie Bernstein realized how special they were, and created a Strnad collection in the Archives. After the Museum became a reality, the dresses and letter were central to the Museum's permanent exhibit. Docents always stop and discuss this powerful story and its implications on the loss of talent and the Holocaust. One early visitor commented, "You know you could do so much more with those dresses." "Like what?" we challenged. "Make them," she countered. *That was the birth of this exhibit.*

For the Museum staff this seemed like a simple prospect. Here are the designs–just create them as they are pictured here! While hosting the first rehearsal of the Milwaukee Repertory Theater's production *A Diary of Anne Frank*, one of several cooperative programs between the two institutions, Bernstein spoke with the director of their Costume Shop about the possibility of forging a relationship to realize Hedy's dress designs. When the new director, Mary Folino, came to the Milwaukee Rep, she agreed to take on this project. Folino, with her expertise in costume design, pointed out immediately what the project challenges were: although the sketches were detailed, there were no technical specifications as to what materials should be used; there were no patterns; the sketches did not show the backs of the dresses; and finally, the Costume Shop would have to reimagine what Hedy would have intended and what her dress vocabulary would have been.

Jessica Jaeger took the lead in capturing Hedy's vision; she is a First Hand with the Milwaukee Rep, which means she generally assists with pattern creation and construction. For this project, Jaeger's attention to period detail made her

Jewish Museum Milwaukee

Margaret Hasek-Guy screenprints a pattern on fabric.

the perfect team leader. In her free time, she is a USO [1] re-enactor with a large collection of vintage dresses, which served as part of her research. For each dress, she created a "look book" of similar styles, patterns and techniques. She also led the efforts to buy fabrics for the exhibit, soliciting swatches from companies around the country to match the color and feel of each dress. In planning this work, Jaeger felt that the big difference between this and the normal work of the Rep is "historical accuracy. When it is theater it is storytelling, it's how the costumes tell the story. With this it's historical; it's going into a Museum exhibit."

Jessica Jaeger tries on one of the vintage hats used for research.

While sourcing the solid fabrics was fairly straightforward, the question of how to handle the prints arose early in the process. Initially, the Museum staff assumed that we would try to match the patterns as closely as possible to existing patterns, but this did not seem to fulfill the Rep's exacting standards of creating Hedy's Line. Margaret Hasek-Guy, the Soft Props Artisan with the Rep, took on the process of screen printing these patterns, recreating them exactly as Hedy drew them. Of these, the white pattern was the most straightforward, calling for two silk screens to be created with the pinks and yellows (Dress #3). For the blue, red and white print (Dress #7), Hasek-Guy hand-painted the black lines, and tested numerous passes of the screening process to perfect the colors. To get the pattern on the black fabric (Dress #1), which has four different colors in the pattern, Hasek-Guy screened out the color using a chemical treatment. After testing the process of screening the color back onto the fabric, she determined that the only way to ensure the color was true to Hedy's design was to paint in the aquas, roses and blues.

For each dress, the Rep team created two mock-ups to test construction questions– would adding an additional dart or two to a sleeve make it "puff" in the right way? Would this inset be done with pleating or would it be a different material? Each test was evaluated next to Hedy's design to ensure that this was as close to the drawing as possible. The detail extended to things that visitors will never see. For example, each of the zippers in the dresses is from the period in which the Strnads lived. The Milwaukee Rep team created a Hedy Label to finish her line. The team also realized its limitations. The patterned dress under the iconic blue coat (Dress #7) has a pleated skirt. Rather than create pleats like this, they sent the hemmed material to a firm in New Jersey that specializes in pleating.

The roses on the evening gown represented another challenge. In Paul Strnad's letter, he writes, "All the members have lost their employments and cannot find any work. I am helping my wife in shapping [sic] and making artificial lether [sic] and silk flowers, which are much in favor here." These flowers were a way for the Strnads to maintain their livelihood as Nazi oppression limited their economic opportunities. In order to ensure that the flowers were created using the same technology available to Hedy, the Rep enlisted M&S Schmalberg – a New York based company that has created silk fabric flowers for over ninety years.

In addition to taking on the creation of the dresses, the Milwaukee Rep staff also created or sourced the accessories that complete each one of these looks. With each drawing, Hedy added specific details like hats or gloves that encourage the viewer to see a complete ensemble, which she sent to potential American manufacturers. The exhibit would be incomplete without these pieces. Crafts Master Andrea Bouck molded and shaped the hats, again taking on the tricky role of interpreter – which hats are straw and which are cloth? How would this hat stay on the wearer's head? With each hat, she tried to capture the mood of the piece while still creating wearable art. Hayley Jaeger fashioned purses from the same material as the dresses, while the shoes are contemporary brands that look vintage. Black T-strap pumps were easy to find, but purple lace-up oxfords are not (and certainly not perfectly matched to the purple coat dress (Dress #5). The Rep dyed these hard-to-find shoes to create Hedy's vision.

---

[1] United Service Organization: An organization created to show appreciation to servicemen and women that was founded during World War II; this is the time-period that Jaeger explores.

What seemed so simple required hundreds of hours of research and fabrication. The team included eleven people, with varied expertise and roles. This was outside the lines of their normal work of fashioning high quality costumes. "We are not looking at this as making costumes; this is creating clothing," remarked Tailor Jef Ouwens. "A costume is worn by a specific person for a specific time period for a specific play. It has to fit the needs of the play. Clothing is everyday wear. There are different considerations for how things are finished." They were dedicated to realizing Hedy's talent, to finishing these pieces impeccably. Senior Draper, Alex Tecoma described this process to me as "finishing Hedy's Line." He went on to say, "We are honoring someone's memory. In any big tragedy like this, we don't think about the creative lives that we have lost. It's a wonderful way to honor someone's work." The peerless work of the Milwaukee Repertory Theater Costume Shop for theatrical productions generally has a life of two or three months. With this exhibit, they have realized a dream and created something timeless.

Costume Director: Mary Folino
Project Manager: Jessica Jaeger
Senior Draper: Alex B. Tecoma
Draper: April McKinnis
Tailor: Jef Ouwens
Junior First Hand: Leslie Vaglica
Stitchers: Kari Ehler, Carol Ross, Micky Simmons
Crafts Master: Andrea Bouck
Costume Apprentice: Hayley Jaeger
Soft Props Artisan: Margaret Hasek-Guy

Ellie Gettinger has a degree in Jewish History and is the Education Director at Jewish Museum Milwaukee where she directs docents, creates curricula, and plans exhibits and programs.

Top photo: Meticulous tailoring by Jef Ouwens. Bottom photo: Hat design drawings.

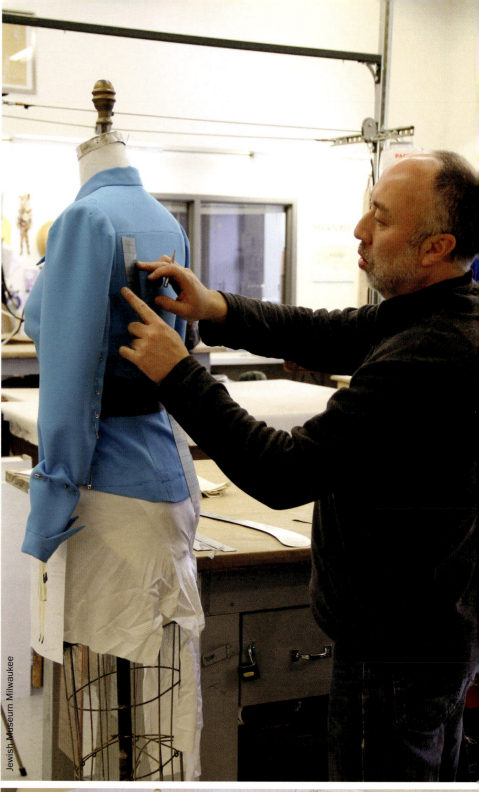

Jewish Museum Milwaukee

Jewish Museum Milwaukee

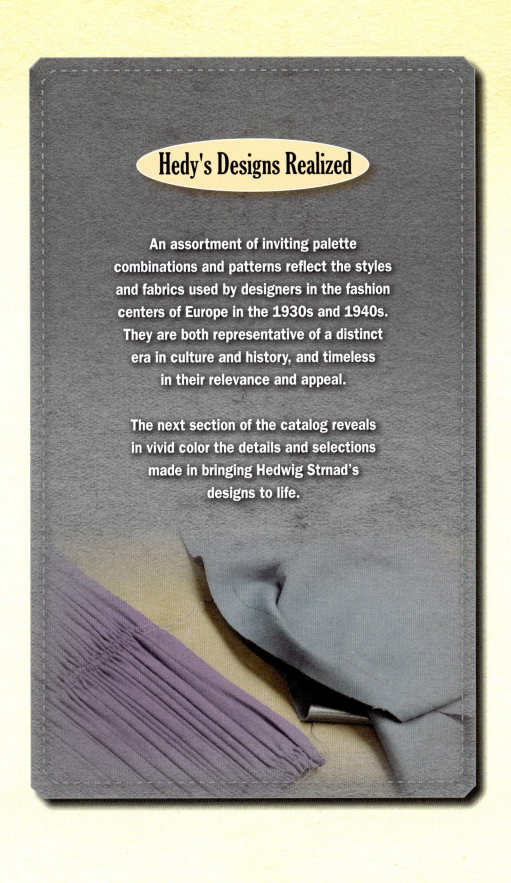

Hedy's Designs Realized

An assortment of inviting palette
combinations and patterns reflect the styles
and fabrics used by designers in the fashion
centers of Europe in the 1930s and 1940s.
They are both representative of a distinct
era in culture and history, and timeless
in their relevance and appeal.

The next section of the catalog reveals
in vivid color the details and selections
made in bringing Hedwig Strnad's
designs to life.

•DRESS #1

SOURCE:
TEST FABRICS, INC.
ITEM #266WB
BLACK CHALLIS, DISCHARGEABLE
100% SPUN VISCOSE RAYON

•DRESS #1

SOURCE:
TEST FABRICS, INC.
ITEM #266WB
BLACK CHALLIS, DISCHARGEABLE
100% SPUN VISCOSE RAYON
HAND PRINTED BY
MARGARET HASEK-GUY

HAT #2

DYED

• BELT #2

SOURCE:
FABRIC.COM
ITEM # 0308634
FAILLE
100% RAYON

• DRESS #2
• BELT

SOURCE:
FASHION FABRICS
CLUB ONLINE
ITEM # 25098
CHALLIS
100% RAYON

HAT #3

• HAT TRIMMING #3
SOURCE: MILWAUKEE
REPERTORY THEATER
COSTUME SHOP STOCK
56% COTTON/44% RAYON
DYED

• DRESS #3

SOURCE:
TEST FABRICS, INC.
ITEM # 266
CHALLIS
100% SPUN VISCOSE RAYON
HAND PRINTED BY
MARGARET HASEK-GUY

• JACKET   #4
• SKIRT
SOURCE:
FASHION FABRICS
CLUB ONLINE
ITEM #24827
GABARDINE
100% RAYON

• JACKET LINING   #4
SOURCE:
BRITEX FABRICS
ITEM# LINING-47-WHT44
SILK WHITE BEMBERG
LINING
100% RAYON

• CONTRAST   #4
• BUTTONS
• BELT
• PURSE
SOURCE:
MOOD DESIGNER
FABRICS
PRODUCT #FW19262
CALVIN KLEIN BLACK
WOOL TWILL
100% WOOL

Coat **5**

• COAT #5

SOURCE:
A K FABRICS

LILAC WOOL SUITING
100% WOOL

• COAT LINING #5

SOURCE:
VOGUE FABRICS
ITEM #32 - KASHATAUPE
KASHA SATIN - FLANNEL
BACK COAT LINING
52% ACETATE/48% COTTON
DYED

HAT #5

• SCARF #5

SOURCE:
FASHION FABRICS
CLUB ONLINE
ITEM # 2H115
WOOL SUITING
100% WOOL

• GOWN #6

SOURCE:
PREVIEW TEXTILE GROUP
ITEM # PV3000-192
ORGANZA
100% SILK

• SLIP #6

SOURCE:
FABRIC.COM
ITEM #
ACETATE BRIDAL SATIN
GRAY
100% ACETATE

• TRIMMING #6
SOURCE: ETSY.COM-
THE VELVET VALET
VINTAGE, C. 1930S
MADE IN FRANCE
86% RAYON/14% SILK

• FLOWERS #6
THAI SILKS
#0036-201
VELVET
18% SILK
82% RAYON

• FLOWERS #6
PREVIEW
TEXTILE GROUP
#PV3000-169
ORGANZA
100% SILK

HAT #7
TRIMMINGS

HAT #7

HAT #7
TRIMMING'S

• COAT LINING #7

SOURCE: THAI SILKS
ITEM# 0Z19-000
CREPE DE CHINE
100% SILK

HAND PRINTED BY
MARGARET HASER-GUY

• COAT #7

SOURCE:
MOOD DESIGNER FABRICS
PRODUCT# FVJ12025
BOUCLÉ
100% WOOL

• DRESS #7

SOURCE: THAI SILKS
ITEM# ZRR-000
PONGEE
100% SILK

HAND PRINTED BY
MARGARET HASER-GUY

• COAT FLATLINING #7

SOURCE:
VOGUE FABRICS
ITEM# MR-COTTON COWDY
ORGANDY
100% COTTON
DYED

• CUFFS #7

SOURCE:
A. J. UGENT FURS

VINTAGE, REAL FUR

• BELT #7
• BUTTONS/DRESS

SOURCE:
PREVIEW TEXTILE GROUP
ITEM# PV1200-WB
CREPE DE CHINE
100% SILK
DYED

• UNDERCOLLAR #8
SOURCE: B. BLACK + SONS
ITEM # 743-B
LIGHT GRAY UNDERCOLLAR
FELT - 12" X 12"
WOOL / RAYON

• JACKET #8
• SKIRT
SOURCE:
MOOD DESIGNER FABRICS
PRODUCT # FW23949
RALPH LAUREN GRAY
FLANNEL
WOOL / CASHMERE

• JACKET LINING #8
• PURSE LINING
SOURCE:
MOOD DESIGNER FABRICS
ITEM # 303061
CHARMEUSE
74% VISCOSE / 26% SILK

• POCKET SQUARE #8
SOURCE:
PREVIEW TEXTILE GROUP
ITEM # PV1200-196
CREPE DE CHINE
100% SILK

HAT #8

• DICKEY #8
SOURCE:
PREVIEW TEXTILE GROUP
ITEM # PV9800-MW21
MATTE JERSEY
100% RAYON

• PURSE #8
SOURCE: [WHALEYS LTD.]
STOCK - MILWAUKEE
REPERTORY THEATER
COSTUME SHOP
100% WOOL
DYED

This is the work of memory: taking threads and stitching them together to give shape to what was lost, and stitching that further into our lives.

– Rachel N. Baum

Suggestions for Further Reading

Books and eBooks

Berenbaum, Michael, *The World Must Know: The History of the Holocaust as Told in the United States Holocaust Memorial Museum*, Second Edition. Baltimore: Johns Hopkins University Press, 1993, 2006.

Capkova, Katerina, *Czechs, Germans, Jews? National Identity and the Jews of Bohemia*. New York: Berghahn Books, 2012.

Epstein, Helen, *Where She Came From: A Daughter's Search for Her Mother's History*. New York: Penguin Putnam Group, 1997.

Greenspoon, Leonard, ed. *Fashioning Jews: Clothing, Culture, and Commerce*. West Lafayette, IN: Purdue University Press, 2013.

Kieval, Hillel, *Languages of Community: The Jewish Experience in the Czech Lands*. University of California Press, 2000.

Guenther, Irene, *Nazi Chic: Fashioning Women in the Third Reich*. Berg, 2004.

Rothkirchen, Livia, *The Jews of Bohemia and Moravia Facing the Holocaust*. Lincoln: University of Nebraska Press, 2005.

Research Websites:

Holocaust Website in the Czech Republic
www.holocaust.cz

Jewish Museum in Prague
www.jewishmuseum.cz/aindex.php

Nathan and Esther Pelz Holocaust Education Resource Center
www.holocaustcentermilwaukee.org/

U.S. Holocaust Memorial Museum
www.ushmm.org

Yad Vashem World Center for Holocaust Research
www.yadvashem.org

Yivo Institute for Jewish Research
www.yivoencyclopedia.org